SMALL GYM BIG RESULTS

Your Complete Guide to **Starting a Fitness Business the SixPax Way,** Living the American Dream, and Changing Lives

IRONHEAD

Ironhead Press
4301 Sepulveda Blvd
Culver City, CA 90230

ISBN: 979-8-9876343-0-1 (paperback)
ISBN: 979-8-9876343-1-8 (ebook)

Ordering Information:
Special discounts are available on quantity purchases by corporations, associations, and others.
For details, visit www.smallgymbigresults.com or email hello@sixpaxgym.com.

To Daniel Rosen, my best friend and mentor,
who believed in me before I believed in myself.

I am now living my dream because of you.

FOREWARD

I wiped away tears as I stood to join everyone in the room in a minutes-long standing ovation. I have invited hundreds of entrepreneurs to speak at my events, but this one stood out as one of the most inspiring I had ever heard. Siavash Fashi had just finished sharing his life story with all of our members at one of my business coaching events, and every person there was inspired.

Everyone listening knew Siavash was an extraordinary entrepreneur doing the impossible, taking a building smaller than the locker room at many gyms and turning it into one of the most successful gyms in the country. From this tiny location, he built a business with revenue comparable to facilities 10 to 20 times its size. A gym that is not only financially successful beyond what anyone would predict but also a gym with a system that creates extraordinary results for its members.

What we didn't know until then was the obstacles, challenges, and life-threatening situations that he had overcome to serve as an example to us all. Through my company Simple Operations, I have coached thousands of entrepreneurs to grow their businesses, but few stand out like Siavash.

If you want to open a gym or make the gym you already own even better, I'm thrilled you are holding this book and reading it now. The unspoken truth of the fitness industry is that most gyms and gym owners are unsuccessful. Many lose money and eventually shut down; some make enough money to stay open and barely survive but rarely flourish or create any level of success for the owner.

People who open fitness facilities do so because they want to help people. They have transformed themselves and want to help others achieve a similar transformation. This undertaking is as much a mission as it is a business. If this describes you, congratulations. Now that you have this book, you will be one of the few gym owners with a clear, executable roadmap to success. You will have the security and peace of mind that come with detailed strategies for overcoming the issues others in your position have faced and the step-by-step process you need to succeed.

Most importantly, you will have the momentum and inspiration everyone I know has felt when exposed to Siavash.

As entrepreneurs, we are that small percentage of the population that gets up in the morning, travels into the future, creates a new reality, and demands it becomes real. We can't turn it off and don't know why anyone would want to. It changes everything when people like us get the right support at the right time. If you have the feeling that the time is now, trust that it is, and have the confidence you have the help you need.

This book will revolutionize the world of privately owned gyms and fitness facilities. There will be those who have read it and created incredible outcomes for themselves and their members and the unfortunate who haven't.

Welcome to the *Small Gym Big Results* revolution and the momentum it will undoubtedly create in your life.

Alex Charfen
CEO and Co-founder at Simple Operations™

CONTENTS

PART THREE
Run

PART FOUR
Grow

PART FIVE
Scale

INTRODUCTION

My life changed the moment I saw Arnold Schwarzenegger's picture in a magazine. He was standing by the beach posing and smiling, looking larger than life. Bodybuilding was illegal in my native Iran, like so many other American sports, because the Iranian government believed it was American propaganda. But when I saw Arnold standing in the sun looking so happy, I knew that was the life I wanted for myself. I wanted to be just like him.

At the time, growing up in a small town called Fash, close to the borders of Iran and Iraq, that kind of life was impossible for me to even imagine. The events that followed made my dream even more improbable: having cancer in my eye and losing my right eye, escaping to America, surviving a year in maximum security prison, being homeless, and working as a security guard led me to my ultimate goal: my dream of starting my own gym.

When I made it to America, I trained at Gold's Gym in Venice, the mecca of bodybuilding. It was every bodybuilder's dream to rub shoulders with the best of the best. I took pictures with them. I was in awe. I remembered reading about them in those banned magazines, which showed them driving fancy cars, enjoying life by the beach, and living in big houses.

But I was shocked to learn how many of my bodybuilding idols were struggling financially.

By the time I got to meet them, most of the champions were retired from competitive bodybuilding. They worked as trainers, trading time for money. Most weren't doing a great job at it. They sold training sessions and waited for clients to show up. Sometimes the clients showed up, sometimes they didn't. For big chunks of the day, my idols sat on their phones killing time.

I found it sad. I remembered them from magazine covers where they inspired millions. To me, they were larger than life. The truth was that the fancy cars and big houses and outsized lifestyles weren't sustainable. They lost it all because they didn't use their brains as much as they used their muscles.

Many people tried to open gyms to keep the old-school bodybuilding way alive, but they couldn't build a profitable business and couldn't scale it. They didn't have a solid system in place. They just rented a big warehouse, filled it up with equipment, and thought that would be enough.

I discovered a better way.

I built my gym from nothing. I used the $3,000 I collected from unemployment at a dark time in my life to start SixPax Gym. I had no money for equipment, no business plan, no safety net—just a burning desire to succeed.

One decade later, I'm living my dream—making millions of dollars out of a 1,000 square foot garage, with a big house close to the beach, a truck, and my Harley. I get to wake up, focus on bodybuilding, and changing lives. Best of all, I get to do this surrounded by many great clients and friends.

Now that I have achieved success beyond my wildest dreams, my next goal is to help other passionate people step into success by showing them the formula I created that allows me to live my beautiful American dream, just like Arnold Schwarzenegger.

In this book, I will show you step-by-step how to build your dream gym. I will share with you all my failures so you can learn from them, and all my successes so you can learn from them, too. I'll cover everything from buying equipment to getting clients, legal challenges, hiring, marketing, training systems, nutrition, pricing, taxes, team building, crisis management, and more. Best of all, I will show you how to change lives and make a great living in the process.

The average gym owner only makes about $30,000 per year and lives in poverty. This is because they lack the right systems and processes. I created a better way.

I have built the most successful small gym in America, and in this book, I will give you all of my secrets so you can do the same.

Starting from nothing, to holding my million dollar award

PART I
Humble Beginnings

CHAPTER 1

HOW I GOT MY START

> **❝** *All the adversity I've had in my life, all my troubles and ob-stacles, have strengthened me...You may not realize it when it happens, but a kick in the teeth may be the best thing in the world for you.*[1]
>
> —WALT DISNEY

Conflict was a constant presence during my childhood.

I was born in 1980, and when I was six months old, a brutal war broke out between Iraq and Iran. It lasted eight years and cost at least one million lives. The war had nothing to do with my hometown of Fash, Iran, itself, but we all felt the impact.

Ideology became a hotbed for conflict. If you didn't declare yourself part of the Shiite community, you would find yourself in a lot of trouble. My family was part of a Kurdish religious minority called Yarsan, so we were bound to run into problems.

The Yarsanian religion preached poverty. It discouraged its followers from gaining material things, as that was a sign of being attached to the world, which was considered a waste of life. It taught that life itself was like a punishment, and we just had to hang in there until we could reach total happiness in the afterlife. So, many of us, including my family, lived in poverty. Getting by was a constant struggle.

After the 1979 Revolution in Iran, we were considered infidels. We were told never to speak about our beliefs with others. Believing something besides what the government wanted you to believe, let alone speaking out about it, could cost you your life.

On every job application, and during every job interview, the first question was always this: Are you a Shiite Muslim who agrees with the government? If you said anything other than yes, you were rejected. That went for jobs and university applications.

All the men in my family and my village were without a job. Everyone was hustling to make ends meet, but the government wouldn't allow anyone to hire them. Their only option was to join the army and go to war with Iraq. Many people had no choice but to deny their religion in order to make a living.

Fash was split in two. On one side were people who supported the government. On the other side were us infidels.

Me at age 8 (on the right) in my little school

Soon, my dad, my uncles, and many other men were sent out to war. It was the only way to make money to take care of their families. My father, Kazem, worked for the Iran Air Force during the reign of the Shah. Once the Islamic Revolution came and the Shah's government was overthrown, the Ayatollah Ruhollah Khomeini, the leader of the Islamic Revolution, took control of Iran. The new government started firing anyone part of a religious minority, like my family.

As war escalated between Iran and Iraq, the new government began arresting people and accusing them of working with America or Israel. People were publicly executed on a daily basis, and the government used this as fuel for war.

At this point, we lived on an Iranian Air Force base built by America during the Shah's time. Since we were the closest air base to Iraq, their jet fighters often dropped bombs on us. Each night, the air raid sirens filled the air, and we'd all have to run and hide.

The windows in my family's shack were taped up because jet fighters passed by our house so low and fast the noise would break our windows. At night, the sky glowed red from all the bullets and gunfire.

We lived in constant fear.

I never knew if my dad would come home or not. Sometimes the military would send him out for 30 days at a time. So many who went out never came back. Every time he left, he told my mother goodbye and gave her instructions on what to do if he died.

As the oldest of four kids, and with my father away at war, I took on more responsibility at home during the war. There was always a shortage of food. I remember standing in line for hours in the snow with wet shoes and a frozen face to buy a loaf of bread. We often sold our meat coupons and relied on rice and bread to get by. My dad's salary was so little that we could only buy clothes and shoes once a year.

At school, many of my friends lost their fathers.

We could leave the base once a year to visit my grandparents in Fash. No bombs were dropped there because the land wasn't valuable to the enemy. It was just farmland.

The village was known for poverty. The government didn't allow larger cities to hire anyone from my religious minority in the area, so they could only survive on the food they grew themselves. The houses were all made of mud and brick. Inside the houses, you could find a little rug and a small stove to heat tea or food. That was it.

The air force base we lived on had strict rules. Everything we did was monitored, including all phone calls and visitors. Not that we had many. Maybe once a year my uncle stopped by for lunch or my grandmother visited for a day and left, but they didn't want to stick around because the area frequently got bombed.

At the entrance of the base, there was a statue of a plane on display. Me and the other kids used to climb and play on top of it. One morning, we went to play and the plane was covered in bullet holes. The Iraqi jet fighters thought it was a real plane and shot at it more than 100 times.

Every morning before we were allowed inside the school building, our teacher gave a speech about how evil America and Israel were and how all our problems came from them.

"If you are not Shiite," my teacher said, "you are an infidel and will burn in hell." It didn't make sense to me—I just knew I wasn't a Shiite, but I wasn't an infidel either.

Eventually the base got too dangerous, so we moved to Kangavar, a city close to Fash.

I was eight years old when I witnessed the hanging of two young men by government forces. They were part of an opposition group that was fighting against the government. It was a public execution. I remember them kicking and shaking. There was no room in my heart for emotion—I had to focus on surviving. My question was always *when would it be my turn to die?*

To make matters worse—yes, even worse—I was getting bullied at school. We lived in a rough neighborhood, and I constantly got called out to fight to prove myself. Once, a bunch of guys threw me into a big barrel of gasoline! I looked different from the other kids in the neighborhood. I had white skin and green eyes. People thought I was soft, so they picked on me. When I told my dad about the bullying, he beat me up and shamed me for being weak and not defending myself.

I wanted to be strong! I wanted to protect myself.

Me at age 12 in front of our house

At the time, we lived with my uncle, but he had to kick us out because my family couldn't afford rent. He had no choice. He had his own four children and was struggling just like us.

We moved back to the air force base where my father enrolled me in taekwondo classes, which I got really good at quickly. I stayed after each class and practiced even more. Every night I went out for a jog and practiced the kicks hundreds of times. I wanted to be the best and perform like a champion. As I continued to practice, I became great at fighting. I was fast and clever, and I could read the other kids' intentions when they put us face-to-face to fight. It wasn't because I was naturally gifted at it—it's because no one else was putting in as much work. I was consistent and disciplined in my approach. I competed at state shows and won in my weight class.

While I was training really hard, my dad was not supportive of me. He worried my training would interfere with my studying. I often had to sneak out through the backdoor to go train.

I started to get recognized, earning the respect of many people in my small town. After earning my black belt and winning state shows, I was invited to compete at the national level. I was a candidate for the national team!

After earning my black belt in taekwondo

But I still had a lot to learn. My dream of becoming part of the national team was slowly dying—not because of my physical ability, but because to be part of the national team representing Iran, competitors had to be Shiite Muslim. I was not. It was a hard pill to swallow, but there was nothing I could do about it. Even if you were the best, you would get rejected if your ideology didn't match what the government wanted.

Eventually, in 1988, the war ended. The country had fallen apart, inflation was bad, and a food shortage left everyone hungry.

My father came home angry after work and often punished me for not studying hard enough or for playing too loud. He beat me with belts, kicked me, and slapped me. He called me hurtful names and compared me to other kids, saying I was useless.

My mother was afraid to stand up to him because he would scream and shout and make a big scene. It would embarrass us in front of the neighbors.

Arnold Schwarzenegger before defending the title for his fifth Mr. Olympia contest in 1974

It was hell outside the house, and it was hell inside the house. There was no break from the pain. Many times, I wished I could die. One day while playing soccer in the dirt, my friend Mehdi showed me a black-and-white photo of Arnold Schwarzenegger standing on the beach in California. I was so fascinated by it. I couldn't believe a man could look like that! He looked strong, but he also looked happy. He wasn't poor. He wasn't in pain. He had it all. In that moment, I knew I wanted to be just like him.

I wanted to learn as much as I could about Arnold and bodybuilding. But, of course, bodybuilding was illegal since it was an American sport, so there were no magazines, videos, gyms, or even pictures of shirtless men allowed.

I started asking around to figure out how someone could get that muscular. Most of the people around me made things up. One said Arnold had to be wearing a padded suit. Another said there was a pill I could take to get huge. But Mehdi heard from his uncle who lived in the U.S. that, to get that muscular we had to start lifting weights.

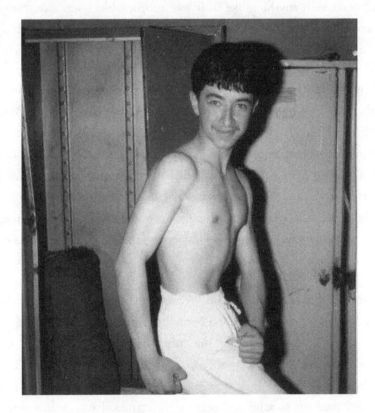

Me flexing after Arnold inspired me!

Mehdi and I started training and lifting in the back of a wrestling gym that had pull-up bars, dips, and a barbell. I worked to train every muscle every day to get stronger. But at 17, I still weighed 135 pounds. Mehdi started getting bigger and more muscular, but I didn't. I realize now it's because I wasn't eating any kind of protein. I was still living off bread and rice.

One day at school, a fellow student told me he had a video of the Mr. Olympia contest. Video players were illegal, but one of my good friends and classmates, Hooman, had one. His parents locked it in a TV stand to keep it hidden, but we broke the lock in our eagerness to watch the video.

I had never seen anything like it. It was unbelievable! I was awestruck by the size of their legs. It didn't make any sense to me, but I *knew* I had to be one of them.

During my last year in high school, we moved to another town in the southern part of Iran. The town we lived in didn't have an art program, which I had been studying at my previous school, so I had to live on my own in a bigger city called Ahwaz, about three hours away. I rented a room with a bunch of older guys who studied at the university. Being a university student was a big deal, as it was very hard to get in. I listened to them arguing about politics and everything happening in Iran. They encouraged me to study hard and to also go to university. They told me it was the only ticket to success for us poor people.

I went to school and studied hard. My roommates knew I couldn't afford much food, so they brought food home from the university to share with me in exchange for me washing the dishes. Some of my teachers noticed I didn't have much money, so they hired me to work for them so I could buy food and clothes. They were building statues of Iranian war heroes, and they paid me to sand and prepare the statues. I was so happy to be earning a salary!

After a year of studying and working, I passed all my exams and got my high school diploma. Then I took the exam to get into university. I feared it may have been a long shot, but I had to try. If getting into university was my way out of poverty, I had to take it. To do so, I had to lie on my application and say I was a Shiite Muslim.

The exam lasted six hard hours. Because the government paid for school, it was very competitive. Thousands of students took the exam to get in. If I wasn't accepted, it meant I had to go serve two years in the military.

A month later, the results were published in the newspaper. Everyone was buying the paper that day, so it was hard to find a copy. My heart pounded as I finally picked one up and started searching for my name. I could feel my hands shake with adrenaline as I read as fast as I could.

There it was: *Siavash Asharfi Fashi.*

I got in! At 18 years old, I was the only kid from my state, plus one of only 65 kids in the country, to be admitted to art university. I called my parents right away to share my excitement. Even with the good news, my dad was not impressed with me. He told me I got in by luck, but I knew in my heart I had what it took.

I quickly realized getting into university didn't mean I had escaped poverty. I didn't have the money to buy quality art supplies, so it was hard to keep up with other students. I saw the gap between us continue to grow. I realized it was an unfair game. Teachers also paid more attention to students who could afford private lessons outside of class.

I saw many talented artists struggling. The high-paying jobs were government related, which meant you had to promote their propaganda—something I could never do. The more I studied, the more I realized we were trapped in a corrupt system.

Bodybuilding offered a good distraction from my everyday frustrations. I kept training and collecting pictures of bodybuilders. I still wasn't gaining muscle or seeing progress because I only ate one meal a day, which the university provided for free. Sometimes in the evening I would eat cookies or a can of sardines to stay full.

At the time, I had no idea that calories or protein were important when building muscle. I'm glad for that, as I couldn't have done anything about it at the time anyway. Knowing that would have just made me sad.

I was on track to being stuck there for the rest of my life. But then came the cancer diagnosis.

One day we were playing in a backyard with an air gun, and I noticed that when I closed my left eye, I couldn't see much with my right eye. Everything was blurry. My uncle told my dad to take me to the doctor right away.

I was diagnosed with cancer in my right eye that had the potential to spread to my liver. The doctor told me there was no cure in Iran, as the country didn't yet have the technology to treat my condition. We didn't want to believe him. His practice was in a bad part of town in the capital city—maybe he was a bad doctor.

I went to a bigger hospital that had many opticians hoping to hear different news. But these doctors shared the same diagnosis with me. They were amazed at my condition, bringing many students in to examine me. Apparently, it was a rare disease.

Everyone around me treated me like I would soon be gone. My mother cried all the time. I couldn't take it anymore!

In an effort to vent out some of my anger and put my art to good use, I started submitting political cartoons to a local newspaper. I considered my-self an intellectual at this point, and like many other students, I opposed the government. Then one day the government shut down 16 newspapers in retaliation—and I was working for one of them! The owner of the news-paper was arrested.

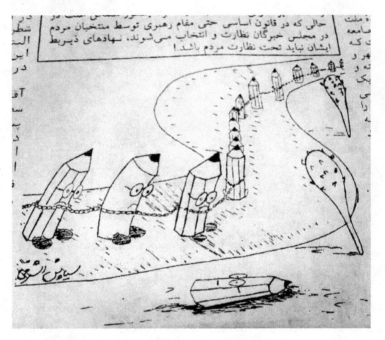

My political cartoon in the newspaper

My job was gone. My health was gone. I could feel my dreams slipping away. I decided to leave Iran. There was nothing left for me there!

I escaped illegally and went to England as a refugee with only $100 to my name.

I bought a phone for $55 and stayed at a refugee camp with hundreds of other people. My roommate was a refugee from Cameroon—he spoke En-glish well, but I didn't understand a thing he said. Despite that, we became good friends, often looking for jobs together. Even though our languages were different, our goals were the same. We all wanted a better life.

Me in England, 2001

Eventually, the refugee camp separated us into different groups to be relocated to different cities. I got on a bus and headed to Birmingham. Everyone in my group was excited to go. We knew Birmingham was one of the bigger cities, so we had a good chance at finding jobs. Plus, people in bigger cities tended to be more tolerant of foreigners. We'd heard many horror stories about small towns where refugees got beat up by skinheads.

But even in the big city, it was clear English people didn't want us there. People looked down on us. They thought we were changing their culture and trying to steal their jobs. They called us names and told us to go back to our countries. Every day people argued on TV about sending us back.

In the beginning, my English wasn't good enough to understand these things, but it didn't take me long to catch on. We weren't welcome. Yet again, my ego was crushed. I spent so much time imagining what it would be like living in America. I thought that by running away from the evil government in Iran and escaping to Europe, my problems would go away. In Iran, they hated us because we were not Shiite Muslims. In England, they hated us because we were not English!

Though I was heartbroken, I told myself one simple truth: I will be a great bodybuilder, just like Arnold Schwarzenegger. I was convinced that once the world saw me winning, it would respect me. It would accept me.

CHAPTER 2

PIECES IN PLACE

The first problem I had to address was my English. I had to learn to speak it—otherwise I would always struggle in the West. I started studying at night by reading bodybuilding magazines. I spent my days working at a pizza shop.

Eventually, I started taking English classes at a college in Birmingham. Most of the other students were English people, so I was forced to speak the language and learn it. Even though it was hard, I loved the vibe. By then, I was around 20 years old. I loved to talk to the girls in class—it was great motivation for me to learn English.

Beyond the language, I learned how to use the internet! I spent hours at the library reading about bodybuilding and steroids. One day, I saw a picture of Dorian Yates, a famous English bodybuilder. Under the picture was an address for a place in downtown Birmingham.

I printed out the map and went to the gym that evening.

6-time Mr. Olympia Dorian Yates and I

As I approached the building, I spotted a huge guy who had a gym belt on him. I followed him to a red door in an alley behind a bunch of dumpsters. I went downstairs and discovered Temple Gym. It was heaven.

This was the gym where Dorian Yates trained. I couldn't believe it! I signed up that day. I even got to meet Dorian. I think my heart rate increased by 40 percent that day.

Temple Gym was a place you went to kill it. There were no easy training days, as we all followed Dorian's routines.

Dorian trained four days a week, doing two sets for each exercise. He went all out for total failure. His style of training was either 100 percent or nothing.

Dorian calculated everything, leaving nothing to chance. His training sessions were short and intense. He was adamant that you could either train long for volume or short for intensity, but you couldn't do both. So, for him, intensity was the name of the game. There was no chitchatting or horsing around during those training sessions. It was a time for hard work.

Temple Gym itself was a dungeon. The roof leaked, and there was no AC or heat. It was full of old-school gym equipment that had specific purposes.

Temple Gym, Birmingham, England

I remember sitting on a porch outside in Iran looking at pictures of Dorian, hoping to look like him someday. He was huge and he never smiled. But in his poses, he looked strong and confident. He believed no one could beat him because it was impossible to work harder than he did. I wanted to be like him more than anything.

Every time I saw him at Temple Gym, all those memories would come back to me. I couldn't believe I was training right next to him. So many top bodybuilders came out to train with Dorian, learn his style, and experience his intensity. I was living the dream.

I told myself I would be Mr. Olympia one day.

One day I was doing a shoulder workout and this big guy walked up to me.

"Can I train with you?" he asked.

"I don't understand English," I replied.

He pointed at himself and at me. "We train?"

I got it.

"Hell yeah!" I said.

His name was Naz. We trained together for many years. I enjoyed spending time with him and being in that gym. I liked the vibe there. We felt safe. No one was trying to sell us anything. It was exclusive. You had to work hard to earn your progress. There were plenty of people who signed up to train for a few months and then left, but some of us were hard-core fans. We became disciples of the gym. We were honored to train in that gym.

The gym itself wasn't fancy. It was about 3,500 square feet—fairly small by other gym standards—and most of the equipment had been heavily used. Everything was loose, but it was all in perfect working condition. The benches had been torn up and taped back together with duct tape. Nothing was perfect, but it was a perfect place.

It was here I learned how to split my training sessions. I realized I didn't have to spend hours in a gym to get stronger and put on muscle. It was all about the intensity. I learned to focus on movement and give it everything I had. I learned about the importance of protein, hard work, and consistency.

Learning about consistency helped in my personal life, too. I created a solid routine for myself and documented everything I did. I knew how much I ate, how much I lifted, and how many sets I did so I could try to beat those numbers in my next session, with either more reps, less rest in between, or heavier weights.

Everything I did had to align with my goal. I never drank alcohol or partied because I didn't want to mess up my routine. Everything I did was geared toward my goal of becoming Mr. Olympia.

I also learned how you could lead others and build a community with your actions. I noticed Dorian never had time to pay attention to each member of the gym, but he inspired us all. He set an example. He made no excuses and set the bar high for himself, and we learned from him by simply watching him go through his journey.

Thanks to one of the guys at the gym, I got a job as a security guard. I still had a hard time understanding all the questions people asked me, but I knew it would force me to learn even more English.

The job allowed me to save up to afford laser surgery on my eye to cure the cancer. Unfortunately, the laser blinded my right eye.

I never talked about my eye to anyone. I didn't want to even remind myself about what happened. After I lost sight in my right eye, the muscle started getting weaker, and soon I had a lazy eye. When I looked at someone, my right eye looked so different from my left eye that I was embarrassed. I thought no girl would ever want to be with me.

In all my pictures, you could tell something was wrong with my eye. I told myself to just focus on bodybuilding to be the best I could be. I reminded myself that I was happy to be out of Iran, and if this is what it cost me to be out of that country, I had no problem with it. I told myself that at, the end of the day, I was still alive and doing what I loved to do.

I never spoke to anyone about having cancer because I didn't want people to feel sorry for me. Plus, it made me feel weak.

Sometimes my roommate would make fun of my eyes and said that when I was on stage the judges couldn't tell who I was looking at. That never bothered me, though—it was my goal to be on stage, and even that joke gave me the confidence that I could do it.

All else considered, things were looking up until something happened at the security job that shook me up and set the rest of my life in motion. One day on the job, we got into a big fight with a bunch of thieves. They shot one of my friends in the leg and ran away. Farid was a powerlifter from Iran—a British champion. We'd often train at Temple Gym together. After he was shot in the leg, he knew his career as a powerlifter was over. I could see it in his eyes—his dream was dead. Then there was another tragedy. Majid, my other training partner, had a stroke while we were at work. I could not hold back my tears as I took him to the hospital. He was paralyzed. A bunch of us raised money to send him back to Iran so he could be with his family and they could take care of him.

I found myself feeling alone. The English hated us, and so many of the friends I made were gone.

I decided to take drastic action. It was time to leave England to pursue my American dream.

CHAPTER 3

GETTING TO AMERICA

I knew I had to make it to America no matter what it cost me. It was the only way my dream would come true. I'd heard that America was the land of dreamers. I'd heard that if you worked hard, you'd be compensated for it, and I loved the thought of that. I wasn't afraid of hard work. I heard it was a land of immigrants and that there were so many success stories of people who started from nothing and became successful, respected, and celebrated. On top of that, Arnold was an immigrant and was able to achieve great success in America because of the freedom. I wanted to be just like him.

I knew I had to take a risk. America and Iran didn't get along, even back then, so I did the only thing I could think of. I bought an Italian passport for €1,500 from a smuggler. Sure, my picture was on it, but it was so obviously fake, I cringed when I saw it. The picture was crooked, and it looked cheap. But what could I do? It's not like I could complain and get my money back from this guy, and I didn't expect him to do a perfect job.

It was all illegal, and I knew that. I had no other choice. I had to go through with it. I had to try. Anything was better than this. I bought a plane ticket, got a clean haircut, and bought new clothes to blend in. Maybe if I went into it with enough confidence, it would work out, I reasoned with myself.

As I got to the airport, my heart was racing. I didn't tell anyone I knew what I was planning because I worried their fear would hold me back. But I was scared, too. I brought a small drink with me as a stress reliever, knocking it back as I headed to the gate.

A woman checked my passport at the gate about 45 minutes before boarding time.

"Your passport isn't reading on my machine," she said skeptically.

Of course, I knew it wouldn't. But I didn't know what to say.

"Maybe try again?"

She checked it again, but I could see it wasn't working.

"Give me a couple minutes," she said and walked away. She showed the passport to another guy, and I could hear my heart pumping in my chest. I couldn't do anything except pray.

When she came back to me, she said, "Son, you have 45 minutes."

She was warning me to leave the airport before I got caught. I saw it in her eyes. I knew she knew my passport was fake, but there was no going back!

I went to board the plane 45 minutes later. As I stood in line to board, I saw security guards looking at me and radioing each other. I ignored them and kept moving forward.

This is do or die.

I got on the plane, sat down, put my seatbelt on, and prayed. Amazingly, the plane took off. I had never in my life felt so relieved! With that relief came a wave of exhaustion. I was so drained I decided I better sleep during the flight so I could be fully alert when we landed.

The relief was short-lived. As soon as the plane landed at Chicago O'Hare, the pilot asked everyone to remain seated. Two officers boarded the plane and arrested me.

It turns out it wasn't even because I used a fake passport. No, the authorities thought I was an Albanian gangster on the run! Why? I guess it's because I was white and had green eyes. I told them over and over again I was Iranian, not Albanian. They didn't believe me until they brought in an Iranian translator to confirm it.

They couldn't believe I passed the security check at the airport. For that matter, neither could I. But because I did, they thought I might be a trained Iranian militant or part of a terrorist organization.

They sent me to a jail near the airport. I stayed in a small cell with six bunk beds and a toilet on one side. I shared the space with several men who were part of a Mexican Mafia. Across the hall there were MS-13 gang members. At the time, I didn't know anything about gangs or gangsters. I figured out they all had tattoos with different meanings and that those tattoos helped them quickly identify other members and their ranks. They were constantly swearing at each other.

I couldn't understand much of what they were saying. I was scared. I was thousands of miles away from home, stuck in jail. For a moment, tears welled up in my eyes. Would this be the end of my journey? Would I spend the rest of my life in this cell?

But then I got a hold of myself. There was no time to be weak! I had to get it together. Despite all my fears, I decided I would act tough.

Two days later, with my ankles and arms chained, I was loaded into the back of a van with a few other guys. After four hours or so on the road, we arrived at a maximum-security federal prison, where I spent the next year.

I wasn't allowed to make any phone calls or use any lawyers. I was regularly moved from one prison to another, sometimes spending six hours chained up in the back of a van. The travel was long, but even worse, it made it hard to make friends.

In prison, friends are important. Everyone there wants to fight you and make a name for themselves. I got into so many fights in those days. I couldn't back down—otherwise people would try to take advantage of me. In a place filled with people from organized gangs with big egos, I couldn't afford to look soft!

I remember in one of the prisons they played the song "Bad Boys" by Inner Circle, the theme song for the show *Cops*, at 5 a.m. to wake us up for breakfast.

Everyone I met in prison was intense in one way or another. Many of the prisoners changed completely and became very religious, but some couldn't get rid of the gang mentality.

My cellmate was one of Chicago's biggest mobsters. He was arrested in the early 1990s. Everyone in the prison was scared of him, even the corrections officers. Despite his reputation, he became my friend and gave me two pieces of great advice:

1.   Stay away from politics and religion.

2.   If there are 10 glasses on a shelf and nine of them are dirty, you end up being one of the dirty ones. But if nine of them are clean and you are the dirty one, someone passing by will clean you up, too. So, when I got out, he told me, I should be sure to hang out with good, honest people.

While in prison, I was constantly being interrogated by the CIA, Homeland Security, and other agencies for hours at a time. It seemed like they wanted to connect me to an event that happened in Italy, but to this day I don't know what it was. It seemed like my translator was trying to confuse me into confessing to something I didn't do.

Most prisoners were scared of me because I was being interrogated so often by government agencies, and rumors went around about how dangerous I could be—my muscles helped on this front, too. Looking back, I think that saved me from so many troubles because no one wanted to mess with me.

After seven months, I got a free lawyer named Max. I was his first immigration case. While that didn't inspire a ton of confidence, I didn't have much of a choice! No one knew where I was, and I couldn't make phone calls to let my friends and family know. I wasn't allowed to send letters domestically, let alone to Iran from an American prison.

Eventually I was able to send a letter out with a guy who was getting deported to Morocco. I asked him to mail the letter to my family explaining I was in an American prison.

Max built a career as a business lawyer, but my case was part of his pro bono charity work. He was a young Jewish guy originally from Russia. We became good friends! I could tell he wanted to help me—I could feel it, but it was hard for me to trust anyone.

One day, I got scared after one of the interviews. What if my lawyer was working with them? What would happen if they accused me of being part of a terrorist organization?

I told my cellmate about my concerns, and he told me he'd look into it. He made a phone call. Later, he told me exactly where my lawyer lived, how many kids he had, and where his office was.

"He's a newbie," my cellmate said. "But he's on your side. Don't worry about it."

And Max was on my side. He put his heart and soul into my case. We went to see the judge, and Max told him my story. After the judge reviewed my case and asked me many questions, he granted me asylum. Max shook my hand and congratulated me. After almost a year, I was free!

Now I was walking on the streets of Chicago, homeless. I had no money, no food, no idea where things were. I was in awe of Chicago and all of its big buildings.

What now?

I got a taxi and asked him to take me to an Iranian neighborhood. He told me he knew of a restaurant he could take me to, but it would cost $100 because it was on the other side of town.

I didn't have any money, so I did the only thing I could think of: I asked him to make a call for me to a former cellmate and friend of mine, a refugee from Syria. The driver made the call and spoke to my friend in Arabic. My friend told the driver where he could take me.

He took me to a mosque where I saw my friend, Imad. He was working at a restaurant then, but he bought me an international phone card.

I called my family to let them know I was alive. Then I called Bralio, another former cellmate of mine. He was from Guatemala. He became a Christian in prison and spent most of his days praying on his bunk.

He got out a few months earlier and gave me his phone number in case I needed any help. And if I ever needed help, it was now!

Bralio and his family picked me up from the mosque and took me to their house in a suburb of Chicago. He put a mattress on the floor of his basement and let me sleep there and eat food from their fridge. I helped out around the house, cut the grass, and played with the kids. They treated me like family!

I got a job helping out with a house cleaning business. Any money I made I would spend at Bralio's house, buying milk for the kids or getting them a new microwave to help out. I wanted to repay them for their kindness.

In my free time, I went to the library and read about bodybuilding. I printed out hundreds of pages at the library and brought them home to study every night. I knew California was the mecca of bodybuilding, and home to Arnold, so I decided I would go there as soon as I could.

As soon as I was able to get my state ID and Social Security number, I thanked Bralio and his family for everything they did for me. Then I bought a train ticket to California.

CHAPTER 4

CALIFORNIA, THE MECCA OF BODYBUILDING

I got to Union Station in Los Angeles with no place to stay, but I was determined to make it work. I asked the taxi driver to take me to wherever the Persians were, so he took me to Glendale where I rented a room in a motel.

I called one of my friends in England and asked him if he knew anyone in the area. I knew I would need some help to get my life started here. He called up one of his buddies, who showed up at my motel. His name was Sebo, and he was a Persian-Armenian. We spoke for a little while, and he drove me around looking for places to stay around the neighborhood.

I picked up a newspaper and saw many job postings for security guards. I called up a company and was hired to do a graveyard shift in a small guard shack opening the gate for residents of a gated community.

This job was all I had. I worked hard to protect it, always dressing nicely, shaving, showing up on time, and being very polite. I created a log-in sheet for all the residents, and I got to know every car and license plate that entered the community. Soon, I got promoted to manager. The best part was that I could also spend time reading and watching videos to continue studying bodybuilding.

I made $1,250 a month then. I found a little place to rent in Glendale for $650 a month. I calculated every single penny to use for food, gas, and car insurance. I didn't have health insurance, so I couldn't go to the doctor to have my eyes checked. I just worked seven days a week and trained as hard as I could. In between, I studied nutrition and human anatomy, along with other bodybuilders' approaches to lifting. If I had any extra money, I spent it on a chiropractor or a massage.

I was loving life!

I was finally where I wanted to be, doing exactly what I wanted to do. I hired a nutritionist to help me get ready for my first bodybuilding competition. I learned so much about food in the process.

At the time, I was training at Gold's Gym in North Hollywood. It had an old school vibe, and it was on my way back from work, so I went every chance I had.

I started training hard with the intention of competing. A fellow competitor at the gym told me I needed to hire a nutritionist if I wanted to have a real shot. So, I hired a nutritionist, Dave Palumbo, who was reasonably affordable. I learned so much through the process. My body was changing every single day. I finally started to look like a bodybuilder! I couldn't stop looking at myself in the mirror.

Getting ready for my first show, after being in America for 1 year

It was around then I started studying to become a personal trainer. At the guard shack, I studied almost eight hours a day on my laptop, reading everything I could about bodybuilding. I passed my exam and got my certifications no problem.

I took everything I learned and applied it to my own gym experience to see if it was practical or helpful.

Once I tried eating zero carbs for four months. I only ate protein and veggies. I experimented with so many different training systems so I could hone in on what really worked.

I was determined to be the best, so I didn't leave anything to chance. There was so much information out there—good and bad—that it seemed like the only way I could be sure was to try it myself. Separating the truth from the garbage sometimes felt like a full-time job.

For my first show, I was set to look great. I'd spent months lifting heavy weights, cutting out carbs, and doing cardio for two hours a day. I hadn't missed a single meal. Everything was perfect—except for that I took a water pill the night before the competition. That pill made me go from 185 pounds to 174 pounds overnight. It was a huge mistake, but there was nothing I could do about it at that point.

I went to the show white as a ghost. I'd planned to get tanned at the show, but the guy who promised he'd do it canceled at the last minute. Tanning through the show cost $100, and I couldn't afford that on my strict budget. I called my friend Jason from Gold's Gym North Hollywood, and he rushed to the show to help me tan outside. He saved me that day! I took fifth place and came home happy.

Dream come true, competing on stage for the first time in 2009

I couldn't believe it. Here I was competing in America and doing exactly what I dreamed about in Iran. I was driving home with my trophy in the front seat of my car. I put so much hard work and sacrifice into this dream, but it was all worth it in my eyes.

I was ready to take bodybuilding to the next level, but it was expensive. The food alone cost a lot, not to mention all the supplements you need to be competitive at the national level. Plus, I needed to hire a nutritionist and a trainer to make sure I trained intensely enough.

Even with a new job, I was working 16 hours a day, seven days a week, buying nothing but the necessities. I maxed out my credit cards to pay for food, supplements, and my nutritionist. I just couldn't seem to get ahead. But I kept going.

Eventually I received my green card and refugee travel documents, so I decided to visit my family in Turkey. I couldn't go to Iran because I would be arrested. At this point, it had been 12 years since I'd seen my family. I gave my job plenty of notice that I would be gone for a time, and I went to Turkey.

I saw my brother all grown up. My little sister had a baby. I couldn't hold back my tears. Everything had changed so much. I realized I sacrificed everything to pursue my dream, and I still had nothing. I felt like a loser. I left home 12 years ago, and I had nothing to show for it. I was broke, I had no wife, no kids, no real job, no real education. I told them about all the stories and everything that has happened to me since I left home. They were in awe, but I could see it in them that they wanted me to come back home and live a normal life.

"I'm worried about you," my mother said. "What if you get sick or something happens to you? You're alone. You'll have no one to take care of you."

She mentioned a couple of women she knew who were single and might make a good wife for me.

"What is all this sacrifice for? What do you have over there that you can't have in Iran? You need to start a family before you get any older," my father said.

They both thought that if I settled down and got married, I might let go of all the crazy dreams I had.

This was the point of no return for me. I was embarrassed, but I acted like big things were coming soon. On the flight back, I was so sad. This trip showed me I had nothing but a dream. What I needed was a plan.

A friend had told me to read a book called *The Secret* by Rhonda Byrne that explains the power of writing down your desires.[2] He told me about it in the midst of a breakup with my then-girlfriend when I felt sad and defeated about losing her and not yet having a gym.

As I sat on that plane heading back to America reading *The Secret*, I decided it was time to try writing down my goals and making a real plan.

I wanted to start earning what I made at my job in a month—$1,250—in one day. That comes out to about $37,500 a month. At the time, that seemed like an unreachable goal. Even writing it on paper was scary. But that was my goal, and I was going to achieve it.

CHAPTER 5

DO OR DIE

I had started making a plan, but soon I'd have no choice but to take real action. When I called my workplace to say I was back in town, they told me I was fired! I couldn't believe it. I had given them notice about my trip, I filled out all of the necessary paperwork, and they gave me the green light to go. I was counting on those paychecks. I was screwed!

I started applying to other jobs, but I couldn't catch a break. Many soldiers were coming back from the Iraq War and were applying for the very same jobs. They were more qualified than me—and to make matters worse, we were in a recession.

I had no choice but to turn to the unemployment office. I was so embarrassed standing in line. After explaining my situation, an officer helped me to take my case to a judge for being fired unfairly. The officer told me this process would take some time, so in the meantime I looked for other work. I started looking for other security jobs, applying at any company I could find in the Yellow Pages, with no success.

One day, I was hanging out with a friend of mine who worked at a car dealership. He said he could connect me with a friend of his who worked for Bally's Gym in Studio City. I couldn't believe it! It would be a dream to work and train at a real gym. Without hesitation, I went to Bally's and got hired as a trainer. They gave me a T-shirt and told me to go find a client to train.

The pay was structured like this: while trainers were looking for clients and working at the gym, they were paid minimum wage, which was $8 per hour. When trainers were training clients, they were paid $19 per hour.

At this point, I had no idea how to sell or get clients. Other trainers wouldn't help me because they were worried about the competition—they wanted to sign clients up to work with them. I got no training on how to succeed. A certification in personal training doesn't teach you how to handle the business end of things.

I started chatting with clients and walking around the floor giving people tips on how to lift weights and correct their form.

I came across a woman who was reading a newspaper.

"What are you doing?" I asked her. "This isn't a place to read! Come on, I'm going to train you for free."

She smiled and followed me.

I trained her and she loved it! She enjoyed it so much that she decided to sign up to train with me. I was so happy. Finally, I had a client.

I took her to the office, and with the help of my manager, I sold her a package of 10 sessions for $750. I couldn't believe how expensive all the packages were. The worst part of it was that, despite the expense to the client and the hard work I put in to sign her up, the gym would take most of the money, only giving me a small portion of the pay. But I didn't care, I had my first client, and I wanted to show the gym I was a good trainer.

I quickly learned that once a client signs up, commercial gyms don't care about the client's success. The only thing that mattered to the gym was the number of memberships you sold.

Our department manager was stressed out about hitting the monthly quota of sign-ups for personal training. If he didn't, he wouldn't get his bonus and his job would be at risk. His stress trickled down to us.

My approach was different. I cared deeply about my client's success. I knew if my client didn't follow a food plan, she wouldn't see any results no matter how hard I trained her. So, I wrote a simple food plan for her and told her to do cardio 30 to 45 minutes a day. She did, and she lost seven pounds her first week!

All the trainers were shocked and started asking me questions. To my surprise, none of them had enough knowledge about nutrition or even training—they knew all the exercises and how to perform them, but they didn't know how to design a program that got results. That was the moment I realized how good I was. I was mad at myself for not getting a security job, but I realized I did have a skill, and I was great at it. Years of studying and training and comparing myself to the best of the best in the world made me doubt myself because I was comparing myself with the top 1 percent. I realized my knowledge was more than enough to help regular people get into great shape.

Two weeks later, it was pay day.

My first paycheck was $160.

How is that possible? That was $80 a week! How could I live on this?

I started hustling harder and got a few more clients, but there was no way I could make a good living like this. I noticed other trainers were stealing clients from the gym and taking them to other gyms to train them—the clients paid less and the trainers got to keep more because they weren't going through the gym. They had to play hide and seek with the manager, because the only way to make a living was by being dishonest.

I didn't like it at all. I didn't want to be dishonest, and why should I be? I was willing to work hard, but big commercial gym systems are set up to benefit the gym. The clients and the staff are not the gym's primary concern. The numbers are!

Many good trainers started at the gym only to leave, taking their clients with them. My first client, the one who had so much success working with me, even told me it wasn't practical for her to keep paying for personal training. It was too expensive. I couldn't blame her! Later on, another trainer stole her, training her at another gym at a lower price.

The system forced everyone to cheat.

That's when I learned that the big gyms had no interest in helping people. They just want to take people's money.

Big gyms don't care. Big gyms are just a big warehouse full of shiny, flashy equipment. People walk in and copy each other's bad habits—there is no direction, no goal setting, no guidance, and no one cares about you or your goals. They count on you not showing up so they can sign more people up. And of those who do show up, very few of them make real progress.

It was at this moment I decided that someday, when I owned my own gym, I would do it the right way. My way.

When you're a part of a big gym, you don't matter at all, whether you're an employee or a client. You're just a number. But in a small gym, you matter, your goals matter, and your success matters, because when you win, the small gym wins too. Small gyms grow when you get results. And that's the kind of gym I knew I wanted to have someday.

Eventually, my wrongful termination case came up.

The judge determined my employer was at fault and gave me $3,000 in back payments.

That $3,000 was all I had to my name. I *had* to do something great with it. This was my last chance. So, I quit Bally's and decided to strike out on my own.

I found a little storefront for rent in Culver City on Craigslist. It was barely 1,000 square feet and didn't look like a gym at all! It was a hole-in-the-wall building with gray walls and concrete floors. It looked like it could have been a hospital room except for the giant crack in the front door window. From the outside, the building looked dark and empty.

The landlord never spent money on the building, and it showed. The bathroom sink, for example, was dirty and broken. But I knew I could make the space work.

I talked to a young guy named Max whose uncle owned the building. Max asked for $1,900 a month for rent, and I agreed to it.

It would be easy to say I wanted to open up this gym because I wanted to help people. But in the beginning, that was not my main motivation.

I opened this gym in the hope of imitating Dorian Yates, the six-time Mr. Olympia, whose gym I'd trained at when I lived in England years earlier. Yates built Temple Gym with hand-selected equipment so he could train with no distractions. It didn't matter who you were when you walked into that gym—we were all equals within those walls. Whoever worked the hardest was the most respected. I studied Dorian Yates closely, from his articles on training style even down to the clothes he wore. I had all his pictures, books, and DVDs.

He did it exactly the way he wanted it. I wanted to do the same thing!

CHAPTER 6

STARTING THE BUSINESS: VISION AND BALLS

I can't recall his name now, but years ago I heard a Strongman competitor on YouTube say that you need two things to start a gym: vision and balls. I told myself I had both.

When I lived in London, I worked for a pizza shop in the suburbs of London called Pizza GOGO. I hardly made any money working there and slept under the oven at night, but I learned a lot from watching the owner and how he ran his business. The owner loved the name Pizza GOGO. It was a clever name, he said—it's short, catchy, and translates to fast pizza. It was easy to memorize, too. Ten years later, I applied the same principle to the name of my gym.

When I was first getting started, many people told me to call it Fashi Training Center or something like that, but I knew that wasn't going to work. Not everyone can relate to the name, plus I didn't want my name to be the brand. For me, the movement was more important than anything else.

I started brainstorming and writing down different names.

I learned this was very important by listening to Ray Kroc, who worked with the McDonald brothers and franchised McDonald's. In several interviews he gave over the years, he said the name was a big factor of their success—it sounded American.[3] And it doesn't get more American than a burger.

I have always been fascinated by language, and I love listening to old-school rap that tells a story, especially how they use words with double meanings. One of my dreams back then was even to be in a rap music video!

For a time, I thought I might call the gym Ironhead, meaning someone who thinks of iron 24/7. But after doing some research, I learned there were too many problems with that name. It was too hard-core and only appealed to meatheads. Plus, it was hard to trademark or get a website with that name because so many other businesses used that name in some way. It also got confusing when brands such as Harley-Davidson had motorcycle models called Ironhead.

But the magic happened! I thought of the name SixPax Gym. It was simple, it was catchy, it was easy to remember. It explained exactly what I offered. I get you a six-pack. That's exactly what bodybuilding does! Better yet, it focused on the movement and the community, not just one person.

I looked it up, and to my surprise no one had the domain. I bought it right away and set up a Gmail account.

Many years later, one of my clients told me if I came up with a tagline that explained my business quickly, I could build a serious brand. So, I came up with the tagline "Small Gym, BIG Results."

Our simple promise

I had a gym with a name. But I still didn't have money for equipment, a business plan, or any idea how things worked.

I started off by cobbling together things like bags of sand, old tires, and sledgehammers. The curious customers who came in those early days didn't seem to mind. They liked me and the gym enough they kept coming back! Over time, I was able to buy some real equipment.

I collected a couple of barbells and dumbbells up to 30 pounds. To find clients, I called all kinds of numbers in the Yellow Pages and walked up and down streets putting flyers on cars. I did anything I could think of to get people's attention. I wanted this to work!

Back then, the floor was made up of gray concrete, and the walls were painted a light gray. It felt like a hospital in there. I hated the color. As soon as I could afford to paint it, that's what I did. I painted two of the walls white and one of the walls red. I loved that combination. It reflected in the mirror and looked amazing. It was starting to feel like a real gym.

My first client's name was Messrob. He was a nice guy, and he always paid on time. Soon I signed up another client named Jesse. He was a landscaping guy. He told me he weighed 523 pounds. He started losing weight fast and got even more encouraged as his friends and family praised him. Before long, he lost 180 pounds!

I signed up a young doctor named Ronnie. He was a young, good-looking fella who got into such great shape at SixPax that all his friends started joining the gym. At one point, I was training 15 doctors! They even looked to me for advice about nutrition. I could tell they respected, admired, and supported me, which gave me confidence.

I was surrounded by a bunch of smart people who wanted to see me succeed. Most of my clients were either business owners, top managers, or in the top of their industry or school. They all had the desire to be the best. That's why they were at my gym.

They gave me advice on business, marketing, accounting—you name it! I was getting the best advice from the best people around, and my gym was getting better for it.

I spent every penny I had on the gym, sparing only enough to put food on the table. The gym looked amazing, and people could tell I was passionate and knowledgeable.

I started buying old gym equipment from Craigslist. I traveled all over L.A., even going as far as San Diego to pick up equipment. I put graffiti on the walls with positive messages and put up posters of bodybuilders and before and after pictures of my clients. I had so many different things on the walls that it felt like a museum.

My mission was simple: teach what has been working for decades. This meant teaching simple, basic movements while including a practical nutrition plan. I promoted nothing but hard work—no fake promises.

In the past, my biggest problem was that I was bombarded with too much information, just like everyone else. The internet has made things worse in this regard. Having too much information made me doubt myself and what I was doing.

I didn't want my clients to feel that way, so I made sure everything we did at SixPax was geared toward the client's goals, training, and nutrition. It was important to keep it simple so they could stay laser focused on their goals and get the results they wanted. Clients loved that they had a simple program to follow and a clear plan to help them get there. They just had to execute it.

CHAPTER 7

BUILDING A BUSINESS

SixPax started to get popular. I was raking in referrals and even training people like the mayor of Culver City and his friends!

Clients continued to lose weight and get stronger, all the while praising me on Yelp and Google in their reviews. People told me I changed their lives. I finally felt like I was doing exactly what I was supposed to be doing.

Being Mr. Olympia was still a dream I wanted to work toward. I worked out hard and spent months dieting, eating only tilapia and broccoli before my next show. I was pumped to take it to the next level, but that meant more sacrifices for my health and my relationships.

Eventually, I realized I was happier helping others train and helping them achieve their goals. It was more satisfying than just working out on my own. I still love competing, and I will do it for as long as my body allows, but I was part of something bigger now.

One of my first clients, Khristopher

I was an expert at losing body fat and gaining muscle. I spent time learning from the best and figuring out how to make bodybuilding affordable and practical for the general public. The SixPax method worked! I tried it on hundreds of people, and they got results.

Clients told me over and over again that I'd changed their lives. When I realized how good it felt to help people reach their goals, I knew this was my calling.

CHAPTER 8

SCALING THE BUSINESS

Clients were signing up quickly, and I was excited. Money was flowing in, but it was also flowing out just as fast. I started to realize the business didn't have much in savings. How was that possible? It seemed like there was always a big expense out of nowhere that popped up and drained a couple thousand dollars here and there, wiping out my savings.

But I ran into the same kind of problems that every gym owner encounters. I was charging per session back then. If a client canceled a session, I would lose that money, plus I couldn't fill that time slot with anyone else because it had already been reserved. I didn't know what to do about it.

One day, one of my clients, Daniel Rosen, helped me step up my game. When Daniel and I first met, he was pissed at me. He had wanted to buy the building I rented for my gym, but thankfully he took it as a sign it was time to get fit and set his grudge aside!

Daniel asked me why I didn't accept credit cards and why I didn't make improvements to my website. I told him it was because I wasn't very tech savvy and didn't know how to do that stuff. But Daniel did know how to do those things. He owned a software company, and he was willing to help me out.

Daniel suggested I train people in groups of three and charge a monthly fee, rather than per session, so I could predict and have consistency with my income and begin to increase it. It felt like a huge, scary change at the time, but I knew I had to do it. If I wasn't willing to change methods, I knew my dream could die.

When I started making those changes, a few clients canceled their memberships. I panicked at first, but Daniel told me to hang in there. Even though I was nervous, I decided to listen and trust the process. Soon, people were enjoying their classes even more! I was able to lower the session prices, take on more clients, and the clients were happy working out in groups with friendly competition.

My income tripled in one year. I couldn't believe it! I started listening to Daniel's advice more often. We redesigned the logo and the website, and I started accepting credit cards. Daniel explained this would help me sign up more clients and keep them paying. Other businesses, he said, follow the same formula.

Daniel also told me that I'd never be able to buy a house if my business was all cash under the table. To be successful and own a home, you have to claim your income and pay taxes. So, that's what I started to do.

In the beginning, I didn't know how to scale my business.

My time was limited. I started my day around 6 a.m. and finished around

8 p.m. My mornings and evenings were usually full and booked ahead of time.

Me with my good friend and mentor Daniel Rosen

Most trainers train one-on-one, and they are never really successful. The only way to make money using this method is to charge higher and higher fees, but the clients never stick around. It's a short-term hustle. Daniel explained to me why this method is doomed to fail.

When you train one-on-one, you get paid by the hour or paid by the session. You're selling your time. You will never get rich that way. You will never get ahead because there's only one of you. It's completely unscalable.

So, how do you make serious money? The secret to wealth is making money while you sleep!

Now, you're probably wondering how you can do that? I'll let you in on a secret: it's called recurring revenue. Are you familiar with this? Recurring revenue is kind of like a subscription service where the customers pay ev-

SMALL GYM BIG RESULTS

ery month, much like a magazine subscription, your cell phone bill, or a cable bill.

It works like this: If you charge your clients an affordable monthly fee and you give awesome value, they will continue to pay you. You add a few more clients every month and your revenue grows larger.

This is NOT a get rich quick scheme. It takes hard work, but it pays off. For example, if you get 10 clients who each pay you $299 per month, that's nearly $3,000 per month in revenue!

Would it be life-changing for you to make an extra $3,000 per month? Of course! But what would it take to quit your nine-to-five? Would it take $5,000 per month? How about $10,000 per month? All that takes is 34 clients paying you $299 per month.

What about getting to that million-dollar mark? The math is really simple. You just add more clients. Once you have 279 clients paying you $299 per month, that's a $1 million.

That's exactly what I did. Once we got our processes down, we got there quickly.

✖ PROBLEM 1

In the beginning, I was training one person at a time. That means one person took up the whole 1,000 square foot space. Even if I raised my prices, even doubling the amount I charged, I would still have the same problem. Maybe my income would go up, but the type of client I worked with would have to change. My market would shrink because only a few could afford it. So, how could I change this?

✔ Solution

I started training three people at a time and I began to call this "semi-private" training. I trained up to six people at a time with help from an assistant. That tripled my income, and nothing needed to be changed. I was still able to serve my clients in a semi-private fashion, but I was able to make more money—meaning the gym could be more sustainable and I could hire more help.

I was worried at first that my clients wouldn't like it, but they loved it! There was less rest and talking between sets; we worked out non-stop. My clients now had some friendly competition who could also inspire them.

✖ PROBLEM 2

I was charging per package, per session for 12, 24, and 36 sessions.

Usually, people started out buying 12 sessions. When they realized they liked my training style, they upgraded to 36 sessions.

Let's say the client buys the 36 sessions and decides to come twice per week. Great. Let's break that down. That means the client's next payment is four and a half months later if he shows up without any cancellations and everything goes perfectly, which usually doesn't happen.

✔ Solution

Charge your clients a recurring monthly fee. That makes things more flexible for your client if they have to cancel a session because of work, family, sickness, or whatever other life problem comes up, but it also allows you to have consistent predictable income.

My style of training requires two or three days of training maximum per week because of the intensity and time needed to recover.

So, I started selling two different kinds of packages. One package was for up to eight sessions a month, or twice a week. The other was for up to 12 sessions a month, or three times a week—and the important part was that the sessions do not roll over to the next month.

By doing this, I was able to drop my prices per session, too, train far more people, and make a lot more money.

✖ PROBLEM 3

For my first four years in business, I only accepted cash and checks. I was scared of collecting credit card information, and I worried about all the fees you had to deal with when you decided to accept credit cards. I was already charging less than other trainers in the area, and I feared the fees would cut into my profit.

Looking back, I can't believe I survived using that system for so long! People trusted me, and that was it. People invested a lot of cash up front for SixPax training, but not everyone could do that! I was missing out on some serious business.

✔ Solution

I found a way to automate recurring credit card payments and have everything in one place by installing Mindbody software. This allowed me to schedule people online, keep track of their payment history, send reminders, and even set up email automation to nurture leads. Most importantly, I could quickly figure out how much money I was making and keep track of my growth. Now, every morning I can tell how many active clients I have, can predict future growth, and can compare and beat my previous years' growth.

Having everything in a software system made dealing with my accountant and bookkeeper much easier. It also came in handy when I needed income statements to buy a house.

✖ PROBLEM 4

In the beginning, I kept track of everything manually—including every session, waiver, receipt, payment, and client files.

If someone asked what their weight was when they first started compared to now, I had to dig deep into all the paperwork to find it. I have seen hundreds of trainers do the same thing! I've even seen some rely completely on their memory without keeping track of anything.

This might be possible early on when you only have a couple clients, but there's no way you can continue with this method as your gym grows. It's inevitable you will disappoint your clients. Plus, if something goes wrong, and you don't have the files, you could end up in court.

Once, a woman named Nancy came into my office with tears in her eyes. She felt defeated and unworthy, and she was frustrated with feeling like she wasn't able to make progress. I searched through all my paperwork and found her first day assessment information. She'd lost 15 pounds and her body fat dropped 8 percent since she started with the gym. She *had* made progress. She'd come so far from where she started. Reminding her of how far she'd come was just what she needed.

Nancy left my office with a big smile. Imagine what would have happened if I hadn't been able to find her file! I would have been embarrassed, and she would have been discouraged. She needed me to come through right then and there! Thankfully, I was able to.

Another time, one of my clients asked to see the waiver they signed. We had thousands of them! Imagine what could have happened if I couldn't find it. That could have opened me up to a lawsuit.

✔ Solution

I converted everything to digital. All our waivers are now done on an iPad and saved in the cloud. With a quick search you can find any client from any period of time.

I typically save all the information I collect on a client, including their schedule, their body fat, and their progress. That way we can go back and see what improvements have been made, what's worked, and what we can do differently.

You don't have to go with fancy, complicated software! You can keep it simple and practical. I use an app called SignNow for waivers and store client information using the Mindbody software.

CHAPTER 9

MY FIRST PIECE OF EQUIPMENT

When I first started out, I didn't have much money to buy equipment, let alone to buy good rubber mats for the gym. At the time, they were out of my budget. I looked into carpeting the cement floors, like I'd seen in many commercial gyms, but then I remembered how dirty and stinky those floors could get. There's no way I wanted my gym to be like that!

When one of my first clients, a pharmacist named Dr. Jacob came into the gym, he looked around and saw sandbags and old tires instead of traditional equipment.

"What kind of gym is this?" he asked.

"Join my gym and I'll get you in great shape. I promise," I said. "With your money, I'll buy mats."

He laughed, and he paid.

Now I had $600 to work with!

My grand opening with odds and ends that I found for free

Rico, the general manager at Gold's Gym in North Hollywood told me the gym was getting rid of its old floor and replacing it with a new one. He told me I could buy the old floor off him if I wanted. It was perfect!

I took a bunch of the mats to cover the 1,000 square feet of the gym. It was a pain in the neck to lay it down because it was so thick—we had to cut it inch-by-inch. (By the way, thanks to Jeff, Gautam, Saba, Jesse, and Vini for that!). But it was perfect for the gym.

When Dr. Jacob came into the gym next, he couldn't believe it. I told him I kept my word, and he loved it. That's the moment I realized I could engage clients and make the gym feel like home for them.

He was invested. He knew he was contributing to the gym's growth, and he felt proud that others would benefit from using those mats. Dr. Jacob and all of my first clients helped build the gym from the ground up—literally.

With the mats in place, I could now slowly begin to invest in equipment that would make noise since the mats absorb the impact and the sound. I just had to bring enough people in to make that happen.

It was time to start working on developing a real, old-school bodybuilding gym. To do that, I needed to come up with the exercises.

CHAPTER 10

MY SUCCESS

> **66** *If you're not making someone else's life better, then you're wasting your time. Your life will become better by making other lives better.*[4]
>
> —WILL SMITH

When I first came to America, I wanted to be just like Arnold Schwarzenegger. I wanted to be Mr. Olympia. I learned everything I could, and along the way I realized I could use what I learned to help change lives.

As SixPax grew, I had no choice but to grow along with it. I spent so many sleepless nights full of doubts, fear of failure, and excitement. I never would have experienced all that without SixPax.

My hard work paid off.

SixPax is doing fantastic as a business. As it stands, I have a team of six people—true believers—who love being at the gym and love helping people. I am constantly hearing from my team and clients alike how SixPax has changed their lives and given them fuel to push themselves harder at the gym and in life.

After spending years training thousands of people and hustling to get the word out about the gym, I'm now well-known in Culver City.

I came to America searching for the American dream, and now I'm living it.

Now I want to share those blessings with you and encourage you to take the first step to open your own small gym, serve your community, change lives, and achieve financial freedom. May this be part of you building your American dream!

The four-time Mr. Olympia, Jay Cutler, at SixPax Gym

PART TWO
Start

CHAPTER 11

YOUR SUCCESS AS A GYM BUILDER®

gym builder

[gym build·er] *noun*

> Person who is motivated to build a successful and profitable gym from nothing, to change lives and make an positive impact in the world.

You may be asking yourself this question: Can I own a small gym even if I don't have a background in fitness? Yes. Yes, you can.

Over the years, I've noticed a surprising fact. It's often much easier to take a person with no background in fitness and turn them into an excellent trainer in a matter of months than it is to take someone with a bunch of experience and build them up from a bad foundation.

I build up my trainers correctly. We start with the proper foundation and build good habits right from the beginning. That's much easier than undoing years of bad habits. When I consider bringing new trainers onto my team, I look less at their experience and more at their intention.

The most important thing about being a gym owner is your intention. If you are passionate about helping people change their lives for the better and you practice what you preach, you are the kind of person I want to have on the SixPax team.

So, where do I have my trainers start?

It all starts with you.

First, ask yourself these questions:

> → Are you in shape?
>
> → Do you look like someone who takes care of their body?
>
> → Do you look like you live the lifestyle?

Why is this important? Well, if you're preaching it, you better practice it. That doesn't mean you have to be already be super fit. The easiest way to start is to follow the training method and the nutrition method I teach throughout this book. Flip to Chapters 16 and 17 on training and nutrition to learn more—and if you follow them, in a short time you will start to see results and have a boost in confidence. This will help you as you work to train your clients in the future.

Once you start your gym, being in great shape will help with marketing. Your body will serve as your business card. People will be able to take one look at you and know you are committed.

Second, take a moment to check your mindset and your approach.

Most gym owners get burned out and want to quit. A big part of this is the nonstop hustle—the constant cycle of finding new clients, signing them up, and losing them. Another big part is the salary. Average gym owners work long, hard hours—sometimes seven days a week to keep the door open—only to make $30,000 a year and live in poverty.

The trick to success, though, isn't just working harder and running yourself into the ground. It's working smarter.

When I studied for my certification to become a personal trainer, I realized the course didn't cover any of the practical stuff you need to know for running a gym in the real world. The courses had an impressive amount of information on how muscles work, but nothing about how the business of personal training works.

My goal with this book is to help you avoid two major traps.

The first is the trap of the fake guru. There are so many people online in the marketing world who have never run a gym before, yet they have no problem advising trainers on how to run their gyms and their business. But beware, because many of the gimmicks they recommend end up destroying trainers' reputations.

The second trap is the temptation for small gym owners to run their gym like a big commercial gym. The result is always disastrous. Gym owners who go this route think they need more space than they do, so they rent a place they can't afford, buy too much equipment, and hire more staff than they need. To make ends meet, they have to hustle even harder—and they may not even break even, let alone have money to put into savings for unexpected events.

These things happen to gym owners because there isn't a good, predictable, teachable system in place owners can use to scale their business.

That ends now, with my system.

Let's start first with how you can get into shape and how you can help others do the same.

Client testimony: *Abby Skinner*

I met Siavash a year ago, and from the moment I met him he became one of my favorite people. He's someone I look up to, and I knew he would become a lifelong friend. He was larger than life to me and I was so impressed with him. He had overcome so much in his life and now he owned his own wildly successful gym!

Earlier this year I lost my job and I was devastated. I loved my job and I had no idea what to do next. When Siavash found out, he told me it was time to open my own gym.

Something told me he was right but I was really scared. I love lifting and fitness but I had no idea how to run a gym! He told me not to worry and promised he would help me. He believed in me when I didn't believe in myself. He saw something in me that I couldn't see, yet.

True to his word, Siavash helped me every step of the way. He sent me an unpublished draft of this book to read and use as a guide to running my gym!

I read this book cover to cover, followed his advice and opened up my own private gym in my garage at home, with a goal to teach women how to lift weights.

It turns out he was right! I made a few posts on social media and women began reaching out to me to come to my little gym! After only a few weeks I had 20 clients, and now a few months later I have 40 clients and I'm making more money than the job I was fired from!

The most valuable lesson I learned from this book was how to build a movement, and it's working. Girls are loving the community that I'm building. This has changed my life, and I'm so proud of the impact that I'm making in other women's lives.

Siavash has built an absolutely incredible community with SixPax. I will forever appreciate him for his support and am beyond grateful to be a part of the SixPax community, even from a distance!

Abby: in her private gym in her garage at home

CHAPTER 12

EQUIPMENT IN'S AND OUT'S

When you're just starting out, be careful about what equipment you buy. Don't worry about buying fancy gym equipment, new gym equipment, or even matching gym equipment. But you do want the equipment to work properly.

In the early days, I saw what looked like a good deal on Craigslist for equipment: $2,500 for 10 pieces! They looked brand new with great upholstery.

But when I started training people, I realized what a big mistake I made. None of the equipment worked right and the weights weren't accurate. Clients asked me how much they were lifting, and I didn't know.

I put those pieces of equipment up for sale, but no one bought them, even when I reduced the price. I tried to give them to the Salvation Army, and even the Salvation Army wouldn't take them. Eventually I gave them away for free to a guy selling gym equipment down the street just to get rid of them.

I started studying gym equipment and learning from other gym owners about good brands and what to look for when buying equipment.

Some of my favorite brands now include:

- → Nautilus
- → Hammer Strength
- → Body-Solid Leverage
- → FreeMotion
- → Flex Fitness
- → Cybex
- → Tuffstuff Gym Equipment

Brand names don't really matter as long as you have commercial-built equipment and it's not too bulky.

When buying equipment, don't rush the process. Be patient. Buying the wrong equipment and trying to sell it again is always a pain, and in the process you'll lose money.

When buying used equipment, don't negotiate price over the phone. Go down in person with a truck and cash in your hand. Be reasonable, and make it a win-win. You can even tell them your story and your plan. People generally love to support bootstrappers. They will root for you and help you out!

I also learned that when buying cardio machines, it's important to look for models that you can still buy parts for so you can replace those parts as they break or wear out over time.

I started off buying used gym equipment from Craigslist. I traveled all over L.A., and even to San Diego, to pick up equipment. First, I collected a couple barbells and dumbbells up to 30 pounds. They were beat up and used, but they worked great. Eventually I was able to buy a few plates and small mats to use for sit-ups or stretches. Craigslist and other auction sites were a good place to start, but I learned building relationships with other gyms was a great way to come by equipment, too. If other gyms are doing upgrades, selling equipment because it doesn't get used, or getting rid of working equipment for whatever reason, they may be willing to sell it to you for a discount.

That's how I was able to finally buy rubber mats to cover the gym floor!

I started buying two pieces of gym equipment at a time and slowly built up my collection. I didn't have to take out a loan, get into debt, or go broke using this slow and steady method.

WHAT EQUIPMENT TO BUY

If you're just starting your gym and you're on a budget, don't worry that you must have all the gym equipment at once. You don't. The SixPax method focuses on getting results with minimal equipment. So you can build up your collection a little at a time, just like I did.

Here are what I consider to be the "must-haves" for every gym:

> → A set of dumbbells up to 50 pounds
>
> → A squat rack

→ One 25-pound barbell

→ One 45-pound barbell

→ One hex bar

→ One adjustable bench

→ Two 45-pound plates, four 25-pound plates, four 10-pound plates, four 5-pound plates

→ TRX bands

During the COVID-19 pandemic, when I only had the option of training outdoors, I only used the equipment above and was able to scale my business to one million dollars. It took me full circle, reminding me of how I started with so little.

If you take your time and do your research you can buy the whole set from someone who is getting rid of the equipment to free up clutter in their home. Remember, the Salvation Army and Goodwill won't take gym equipment. So many times I was offered the equipment for free, just so people could avoid having to pay someone to haul it away.

Ready to invest more? Here are my next equipment recommendations:

→ Additional dumbbells 50 to 100 pounds

→ Another 45-pound barbell

→ Two EZ Curl barbells

→ One treadmill

→ One elliptical

→ Another adjustable bench

→ One decline bench

→ One hyperextension bench

→ Kettlebells: 15 pounds, 25 pounds, 35 pounds, 45 pounds, 55 pounds

→ Mirrors. Put mirrors on a couple of the walls to make your small place look bigger. Plus, everyone loves to check out the sick pump they get from training.

→ Thick mats for the floor so you can drop weights without causing damage. Plus, it absorbs sound. Don't use carpet, because it's too hard to clean.

Once you have enough clients and space, purchase the following:

→ Leg press

→ Leg extension

→ Cable crossover

→ Leg curl

→ Smith machine

→ Lat pull-down

→ Stairmaster

WHY BIG GYMS HAVE SO MUCH EQUIPMENT

You may have noticed that big gyms have a ton of equipment. Why? That equipment is easy to use, so there's a lower risk of injury. That means the gym owner has less liability.

Having that many machines makes a trainer's job easier. There's no setup involved. But that also means the client is pushing against a path of least resistance, working on a very isolated group of muscles.

That's perfect for a big gym. If you just joined and you have no idea how to train, you'll just walk around and copy others. That means commercial gym owners don't have to watch you and they don't need to hire as many staff members.

I had none of these issues. I watched my clients all the time. I trained them with simple movements, and I could see immediate changes in people who used free weights. That method targeted a few muscles at a time, so it was harder and more taxing, which equaled faster results!

SELLING EQUIPMENT

I have sold many pieces of gym equipment online. If you have the space, be patient when it comes to selling.

Don't drop your price too fast. Instead, this formula seems to work: If something doesn't sell in two weeks, drop the price around 10 to 15 percent. Wait another two weeks. If it still doesn't sell, drop the price another 10 to 15 percent.

If you don't have the space and you have to rent storage to make it work, sell those pieces of equipment ASAP. Price them lower than fair market value to get rid of them and move on. Remember, while it doesn't hurt to make good money off the equipment you spent good money on, you are a gym owner—you're not in the business of selling equipment.

If a piece of equipment in your gym doesn't get used on a daily basis, or if you haven't used a machine or bar in six months, get rid of it. Make room for something else or just leave the spot empty. Your gym will look bigger and cleaner for it.

WARM-UP

Each session must begin with a warm-up! Don't leave clients to do this part by themselves, because they usually ignore this part and jump right into a training session. This is dangerous because it can increase their chance of injury.

I didn't want to start my sessions with boring stretches or boring warm-ups, so I got a couple of 10- and 12-pound sledgehammers and a $60, 300-pound tractor tire from Craigslist. I like to have clients start there.

Sledgehammer and push-ups: the perfect warm-up!

Maybe the client is angry after a long day at work or is coming in to train after a lazy day at home. We start the session by hammering the tire with 10 reps each side. Then I have them do two sets of 15 push-ups for three to five minutes on the tire. Clients love it! This has become our staple.

It also works as a great marketing tool because we do this outside, so people see us hammering the tire as they drive by, and they think it's interesting. Many clients have told me they joined the gym because they wanted to hammer that big tire.

It's a great warm-up tool. It puts people in the right mindset as they begin. It clears their minds and brings them into the present moment because they have to really focus on the movement. Then they're ready to go hard!

STAY IN THE PRESENT

Have you ever ridden a motorcycle? I ride my Harley every Sunday and go through Malibu Canyon. After each ride, I feel amazing. It's like meditation for me. You know why? It's because I have to be present every single second—otherwise, I'm risking my life. I constantly scan the road, pay attention to the engine and the brakes, gauge my distance, and calculate my next move.

This is exactly the kind of feeling I want you to bring to your clients even as the warm-up begins. Keep them in the present by engaging them in a focused movement. Make sure they are paying attention. If they aren't, make sure you stop to explain to them how and why it is so important they do so.

Trainers must be present, too. As a reminder, you should never be on your cell phone when training clients. Not even during the warm-up.

Clients are paying for your expertise and your full attention. That should be reason enough to stay off your phone, but it's important to remember that weight lifting can be dangerous if you don't perform the exercises correctly.

Many people don't want to lift weights on their own because they are afraid of hurting themselves, so they hire you.

It's disrespectful and unprofessional to be seen on the phone while training clients. They will start to feel ignored and unimportant. While clients may not complain about phone use, they notice it. And they won't hesitate to leave you for another trainer who cares about them and respects them enough to pay full attention at all times.

Never let their minds wander by giving your clients too much of a break, talking to them for too long, or explaining too much. You must keep the session moving.

KEEP IT SIMPLE

Keep it simple and fun. You want to make sure the warm-up isn't too challenging and everyone can do it. You don't want your clients to feel like a failure right from the start!

CHAPTER 13

TRAINING

At SixPax, we value intensity over the length of the session. Much like a sprinter, if you go hard, you can't go for long. We create hard sessions that last exactly 30 minutes.

While my clients are warming up, I quickly ask about everyone's diet and cardio. I don't want them to feel guilty about it—I just want to help them stay accountable and conscious of those things.

ABOUT REPS

Before I get into the full training sessions, we should talk about reps. We want to keep the reps around 15. Why? Most beginners have no idea what muscles they are targeting, and believe it or not, most of them have never trained these muscles before. This may be completely new to them. It takes almost 10 reps for them to develop the right mind and muscle connections and another five to feel that good burn.

So, keep the weight light enough that your clients can complete 15 reps, but heavy enough that the last few reps will be challenging.

The first few reps may not look perfect. Don't panic! Slow down the movement and let your client experience the feeling. Giving too much explanation or instruction won't help. Just like a taste of sugar, you have to experience it for yourself to truly understand it.

Allow your client to make mistakes and correct their form along the way. Just make sure the weights are light enough that they are forgiving when your clients make those mistakes.

Once in a while, shock their muscles with much higher reps, like two sets of 25 or one set of 50. I like to do this every few weeks with exercises that are safe in case of muscle failure, like curls, leg presses, or leg extensions.

TIP: *Limit each exercise to two sets. Why? When you have two sets, it's easier for the client to give everything they have because they know it will end soon.*

Sets are usually performed like a pyramid, starting light and increasing the weight on each set. Your last set would be the heaviest. Once you are warmed up, you don't need those light sets, and you can go at it as hard as you can. If you do more than two sets, you will be tempted to save a little energy reserve for the third and fourth set. When you know you only have two sets, you will have a different mindset. Again, when it comes to weight lifting, it's all about intensity.

THE PERFECT SESSION

I designed two different sessions, simply called Plan A: Upper Body and Plan B: Lower Body. It's important to keep it simple so neither the trainers nor the clients get confused. I want everything to be clear enough that everyone comes into the gym knowing what to expect.

Choose simple, effective exercises. Avoid things that waste time with set up and adjustments. Stay away from using too many machines.

I've seen many clients who worked with other trainers but couldn't do regular push-ups or a straight barbell curl. Why? Their other trainers relied too heavily on machines. They have their place, of course, but when you are specifically trying to build strength, machines aren't the best method.

Machines work well for commercial gyms that want to reduce the risk of injury, so they don't have to hire experienced trainers or spend time training clients.

Without those machines, you must build their foundation with basic movements.

Plan A's session works out the chest, back, and biceps. Plan B's session works out the shoulders, legs, and triceps. Let's dive in.

As a trainer, the first thing you need to do is make sure you say hello to your clients as they walk through the door. I like to tell them I hope they're ready for the day—it gives them a chance to snap out of their thoughts about work and whatever may be stressing them out to help them get focused.

Remember, you are a coach and a leader at your gym. People look to you for direction and guidance, and that plays a huge part in making for a perfect session.

PLAN A: UPPER BODY

Chest

Start the chest session with a basic movement. I like push-ups best. Then move to exercises such as dumbbell presses. Dumbbell presses are challenging and stabilizing, plus there is very little change of injury. Keep it to two sets of 15 reps.

Dumbbell presses are my favorite because they build a strong foundation, and they are very basic. They don't require much setup, and they don't require you to spot your client. This is an excellent, efficient use of time in a semi-private class.

If instead you had all your clients do barbell benching, you would have to spot every single person to make sure no one gets hurt.

Plus, this gives your clients the chance to get a sense of what they really can and can't handle. Teach them right away that it's okay to go up and down in weight as needed. We want to train and build muscle, not lift with ego.

Here is a simple routine:

Sledgehammer/Tire/Push-ups 2x15

Always start with some sort of warm-up exercise. I like to start off with a tire and hammer and tire and push up sets. Pushups, mechanically, are the same as a bench press. It's a great tool to warm-up your whole body to prevent injuries and get a quick pump. Plus, it pre-exhausts the muscle, so once you move to the bench press, clients won't be able to go as heavy, which prevents injuries and saves your joints in the long run.

Warming up with sledgehammer and push-ups on a tire

Abs Exercise or Chest Muscle Stretch for One Minute 2x20

Two sets of 20 reps, abs, or stretching chest muscle for one minute.

Between sets, you must either do some sort of abs exercise or stretching. Stretching between sets is awesome! I learned this from Dorian Yates when I was training at Temple Gym in Birmingham. We were always encouraged to stretch between sets because it increased the pump and stretched the fascia, so it made room for muscle growth and prevented injuries.

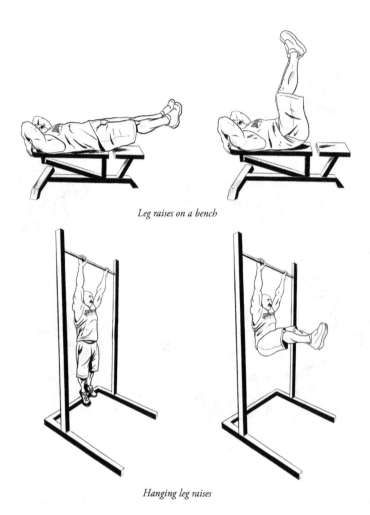

Leg raises on a bench

Hanging leg raises

Flat Dumbbell Bench Press 2x15

I love this exercise! It's easy to explain to clients and easy for everyone to figure out how to perform. Give your clients tips, such as not locking their elbows, because we are trying to keep the tension on the muscle with the correct range of motion, all while keeping the weight light enough so they can do around 15 reps. If they can do 20 reps, the weight is a little too light.

Superset (i.e., alternate) with two sets of 20 reps of crunches.

Flat dumbbell bench press

Superset Crunches 2x15

Superset all your exercises with some sort of abs training in between sets. For example, after a set of bench presses, right away move on to leg raises for 15 reps then back to benching. By doing this your chest muscles are resting, and you can work on the abs. Make sure those exercises aren't hard enough to take the intensity away from the main exercise, which is the bench press. I like supersetting because we can squeeze a lot more exercises in 30 minutes. Usually you need 30 to 60 seconds to recover from the set, so standing around checking your phone or chitchatting doesn't help. You can build great cardiovascular strength by doing this as well, but you must make sure the second exercise that you choose is not too intense, so it doesn't take away from your main lift.

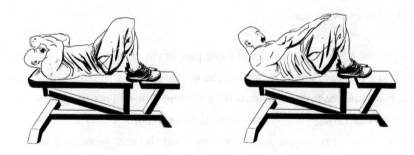

Superset with crunches

Incline Bench Press Dumbbell/Barbell 2x15

Choose another exercise for the chest. I like to do another press movement because my main goal is to build strength and mass at the beginning of the training plan. You can even do flies or flat bench on the floor. Just keep it simple and try to not change the exercises often so your clients can get stronger and measure their improvement. If you start rowing with 50 pounds, and a few weeks later you're rowing with 80 pounds, it's very rewarding.

Between the two sets, do a 15-rep abs exercise for 15 reps. I usually either do leg raises on the bench or crunches.

TIP: *The negative part of the movement is very important.*

When lifting weights, each rep consists of a positive and negative phase. For example, imagine you're doing a bench press. When you lower the bar on your chest, you are doing negative work on the bar. When you push the bar above your chest, you are doing positive work on the bar.

When we lift, what often comes to mind is the big push—the positive work. But remember, the negative part of the movement is the part that damages the muscle the most. You can see most Olympic weightlifters drop the weight from the top when they are training because lowering the weight makes the recovery harder.

But we want to take advantage of every part of the movement. We want to make the exercise harder by moving the weight in a slower, controlled manner, time under tension. Make sure to remind your clients to control the weight at all times. They are the boss, not the weights. For example, when you are bench pressing, control the weight on the way down and push it back up with explosiveness. Explode on positive and go slow and in control on a negative. By doing this, you also reduce the chance of getting injured.

Incline dumbbell bench press

Incline barbell bench press

Back Attack

Heavy Dumbbell Row 2x15

The staple of every back exercise should be rowing. Rowing builds thick lats and a strong back!

You need to build a strong foundation.

For the beginner, I strongly suggest dumbbell rows. I know everyone will hate it, including you, but it works. It does wonders building back muscles, and it's very safe and easy to explain. What's the worst that could happen? You let go of the weight and it drops in front of you without hurting anyone else. If your client does drop the dumbbell, just have them correct their position and show them the right range of motion. The first few tries might be ugly, but they'll get it eventually.

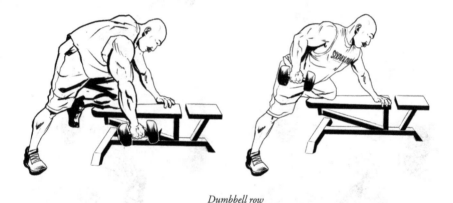

Dumbbell row

Between sets, do another 15-rep abs exercise. This will allow clients' targeted muscles to rest while working out their abs. I use a suspension trainer band (TRX) or pull over or light deadlift.

We use these movements to improve lifting mechanics and build strength to prevent injuries—whether from lack of flexibility or lack of strength.

Many of us spend a lot of time on the computer, too, so we lose our glute muscles because we don't use them. Use it or lose it!

So, if you want your clients to do deadlifts, I recommend starting with the hex bar. You might say that's too much leg, so you need to teach them how to use their legs first. Pay attention to their form, start light, and make sure they are performing the exercise correctly. Have them do hyperextensions, the farmer's carry, or lat pull-downs to build those muscles safely.

Let's move on to arms.

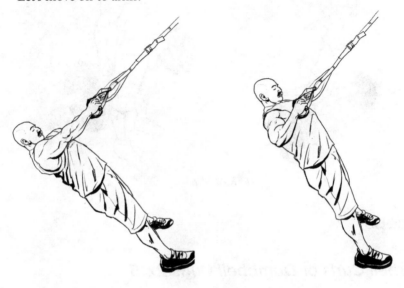

Suspension trainer (TRX) band

Dumbbell pullover

Hex bar deadlift

Biceps

Barbell Curls or Dumbbell Curls 2x15

I like dumbbell curls, especially for new clients. When they use them for the first time, many clients realize how unbalanced they are. One arm might be able to curl 20 pounds for 15 reps while the other can barely do eight reps.

Barbell curl

Superset the biceps with dips on the bench.

Knowledge is power! Now that we know where the unbalance is, we can do something about it.

🏋 **TIP:** *Squeeze the muscle.*

When you are training your clients, make sure to remind them to squeeze their muscles as hard as they can. This will teach them what muscles they are training and will help prevent injuries in the long run.

For the second exercise, I use a standing barbell curl. It's a simple and effective movement; again two sets of 15 reps.

Dumbbell curls

Plank

I always like ending my session with planks. It slows everyone down and lets the client end on a challenge. Encourage them to hold the plank for as long as they can and challenge them to push further every time. It's a great exercise that is both safe and effective.

Plank

After the Session Is Over

Encourage everyone to do cardio. Many people want to jump in their car and leave right after the session, but you can ask them to do 20 to 30 minutes of cardio. People appreciate you not letting them off the hook and keeping them accountable! Don't make people feel guilty, but constantly encourage and educate them to do better.

PLAN B: LOWER BODY

Shoulders, Legs, and Triceps

Push-ups 2x15

Always do some sort of warm-up exercise. Again, I like to start off with a hammer and tire and push up sets.

Shoulder Presses 2x15

I like to start with the basic standing shoulder presses—nothing complicated—using either a barbell or dumbbell. Do not go too heavy on this movement. It's important to be very careful when it comes to shoulders. Form is everything! As soon as you see a client losing their form, either spot them or reduce the weight to make sure they don't get injured. Keep the rep range around 15 reps again. Control the weight on the negative part of the movement.

Between the sets, do jumping jacks to flush the lactic acid from the shoulder to help clients perform the second set better. As a bonus, this keeps them moving and focused on the workout.

Standing barbell shoulder presses

Standing dumbbell shoulder presses

Upright Row or Side Lateral 2x15

Keep it simple by doing another exercise for the shoulders. With shoulders, encourage your clients to feel the pump. Building shoulders is much easier than some other muscles because we have a much better mind-muscle connection with our shoulders compared to our back muscles, for example.

Side laterals are a great movement too, along with an upright row. You can switch them every week—one week upright row, another week side lateral.

Do two sets of abs between the sets, no rest time. They'll rest the target muscles while doing abs.

Upright row

Side lateral

🏋 **TIP:** *Water break.*

I usually allow a water break after completing two exercises or when I am done with the muscle. For example, after your two exercises for shoulders—which normally last 10 minutes—is a great time for a water break. Of course, they can drink anytime during the session, but I like to keep the flow by pushing hard for 10 minutes then giving them 20 to 30 seconds for water break. Then we get right back to it. This way, no one is rushing anyone and no one is left behind. We are all going at it with full intensity and focus.

Legs

Make sure clients know it's leg day by raising hell. When they think of leg training, there must be this mix of excitement and fear—it is so much fun to train legs because you can really take them out of their comfort zone and show them they are much stronger than they think they are. After a great leg training session clients feel spent, happy, and accomplished!

When it comes to leg day, many people want to skip it. Some feel it's not important to train legs. Some women believe that by training legs, their legs will get bigger and look too muscular. And some men don't want to deal with the soreness. But I can't emphasize enough how important it is to train legs. This will boost your metabolism, which will help you to burn more body fat. It will also strengthen important muscles, which will prevent injuries. Believe it or not, training your legs will impact your whole body. Like throwing a rock in a pool, a great leg training session will put your whole body under tension.

Leg day is important. You don't have to train heavy, but you do have to focus on your form and be consistent.

Jump Squat 2x15

Make sure you are warming up properly before your leg sessions start. Again, it's important to prevent injuries.

I always start with a jump squat. You will be surprised at how many people don't know how to squat their own bodyweight, and this is a great chance for you to teach them! If their form is really bad, have them squat on a bench then jump. Give them two sets of 15 reps to warm-up the knees and get their quads ready for what's about to come.

Jump squat

Leg Extension 2x15

This is a great exercise to start with. Don't go too heavy on this exercise, and again, stick to 15 reps for each set. Once every few weeks, go as high as 50 reps on this exercise. It's safe to perform, and it burns like hell. Teach your clients to control the weights on the way down and be explosive on the way up. Teach them to utilize the full range of motion, going all the way down and all the way up. Don't rush them—let them enjoy the pain.

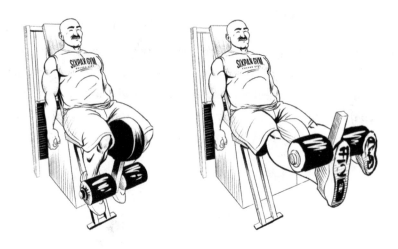

Leg extension

Squat/Leg Curl/Lunges/Leg Press 2x15

You can choose any of these exercises. Keep switching them around and choose one according to your clients. For women, I always give them squats. For men, I usually give them leg presses. If I'm training athletes, I usually give them squats and leg curls.

When it comes to leg training, always keep the reps high. Leg muscles have higher endurance, and in order to get them to respond, you must push them beyond their comfort zone.

After a leg training session, clients are usually out of breath and feel like they can't do anything else. They will want to go home, and they will if you let them! Stay on top of them here. Tell them to drink some water, rest for 5 to 10 minutes to catch their breath, then have them do 30 minutes of light cardio.

Explain to them that this cardio session will help prevent them from being super sore the next day. Treadmills or ellipticals are great for cardio after a leg day session.

Barbell squat

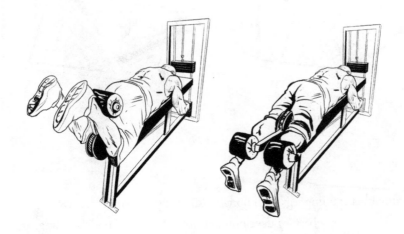

Leg curl

Dumbbell lunges

Leg press

Tips

I remember training legs with bodybuilding legend Tom Platz, even to this day. He holds the best leg development in the history of bodybuilding, and for good reason. We trained for three hours straight.

On Saturday mornings at 7 a.m. we met at Gold's Gym in Venice, and we did only two exercises for three hours. It was all about intensity as we switched between squats and leg curls.

Posing practice with Mr. Universe Tom Platz

I've noticed people do too many exercises with lower intensity. Doing 10 different things for legs to hit all these different angles just won't make that much of a difference for most of your clients. Keep it simple. Limit legs to two exercises but push them as hard as you can.

Once in a while, challenge your clients to a full 30-minute leg session. Make it memorable! When I see my old clients, they always reflect on how hard they trained at SixPax and remember it as a good time.

Overhead Triceps Superset with Dips 2x15

Overhead extensions are another simple and effective exercise! Doing them on a bench is much safer than doing them while standing. If you stand, you are in a stronger position, and you might be able to move more weight, but sitting down prevents you from going too far back, plus it isolates the triceps.

Overhead triceps

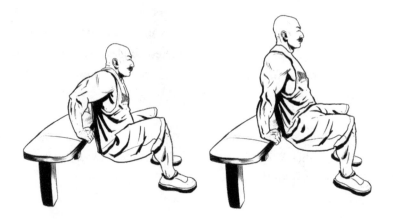

Dips on a bench

TIP: *I love dips. I always use this basic movement for my clients. It's very easy to set up; you just need a bench. It's easy to explain, and it's super beneficial. I recommend having your clients do 2 sets of 15 reps.*

Superset the overhead triceps with dips, no rest in between to fry those triceps!

Skull Crushes or Close Grip Push-ups 2x15

Skull crushers with dumbbells or barbells are another great exercise to build a strong foundation. It's easy to set up, plus clients can make errors without getting hurt. Assign your clients two sets of 15 reps.

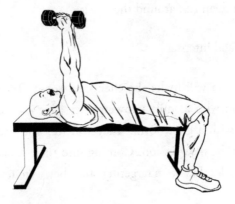

Dumbbell skull crushes

Dumbbell skull crushes

Make sure their arms are fried. Every muscle should be treated with the same intensity!

Last, we end strong with a plank.

TIP: *Always start and finish in 30 minutes.*

Do not cut anyone short.

If you still have a few minutes left in the session, make sure you put it to good use! Do not be lazy and terminate the session even if clients are acting like they can't take it anymore. Make them do another set of triceps or planks, or have them run around the block.

Keep it simple and intense!

The perfect session will make the client feel spent. They will walk away from the session with a smile knowing they gave it everything they had while training with a good form. They will feel safe and hungry for improvements for the next session. Coming into their session that day, they knew what muscles they were targeting, and they were ready for it.

Client testimony: *Gautam Shenoy*

The year that began as 2013 lingered with the remnants of a debilitating back injury that had put me out of commission for more than three months. I struggled to walk, bend, and go about even my daily chores without effort. Even the slightest misstep would trigger my L5-S1 injury and send painful shockwaves through my lower back. That meant another two weeks of rest and a lost opportunity at going about my life.

I had to take some time off, so I visited my family in Mumbai, India. While I was browsing online, I came across an ad for a gym a friend had recommended. The advertisement said all it took was 30 minutes of training, a few times a week to get my health back. Getting in shape was not even on my mind—it felt like a distant dream. So, upon return, I took a drive to Culver City from Hollywood.

I met Siavash that night at the gym—this was in February 2013. He was in the back, sitting at a desk, working away on a computer since he had just finished training someone. As I entered, he greeted me, we spoke, and he did a quick evaluation of my weight, height, and body fat. He even suggested that I could try a free session right there. But I was too scared, and he was kind enough to help me set an appointment.

Thus began a new chapter in my life. Little did I know that this first step into the world of SixPax would turn the page so definitively in my life. When I started doing cardio, I could barely do a minute on the stair machine. I even recall walking through other gyms in earlier years, glancing at the people grunting on these climbing machines, laughing at myself that I could never do it!

It has been eight years and I have clocked hundreds of hours on the stair machine, with or without music. I do not put a towel on the timer because I choose to look at my effort chipping away at that 60-minute goal.

This kind of a mindset that is hell-bent on getting the work in is something I cultivated at SixPax. I truly believe that Siavash is not just a trainer, he is a teacher who imparts a sense of purpose, a sense of indomitable strength to challenge oneself and work through the discomfort, pain, and a mind that wants you to give up. Instead, the heart beats at 168 bpm, bolstering this effort and reassuring me that I have done it before, and I will do it again.

In the early days he kept me accountable by asking me to send a picture of EVERY meal I ate, so he could be certain I was not cheating. If I was not at the gym doing cardio, I had to send him a picture of any machine that I used to make sure I had done the work. This was not pressure, it was about cultivating a resilient frame of mind that compelled me to make fitness my lifestyle, not a boring chore that I dread at the very thought of!

While I worked in multiple offices—be it Pasadena, downtown L.A., or Santa Monica, I would still drive each evening to the gym in Culver City to train or simply to do my cardio. It's been eight years and a journey so rewarding. I have bought every SixPax T-shirt and hoodie in every color each time there is a new one in stock. Not only does it represent SixPax Gym, it represents my journey and the climb of an imaginary mountain that has infinite rises, crests, and mesas. The climb has not stopped since.

I have lost over 100 pounds through this journey. I can squat over 240 pounds, and I do not struggle with injuries anymore. Keeping up with cardio is hard, but I choose to do it because it is for me. I had social anxiety, which I have overcome and today I speak at conferences and am considered a leader in my field of work. This confidence and indisputable sense of purpose is a direct result of the effort I put in at the gym with constant encouragement from Siavash and his team.

Siavash is not just my trainer, he is a dear friend, mentor, and a brother. I see him change lives every day. Be it carving champions out of the Culver City football team, training seniors who have dealt with lifelong injuries, or working with kids with disabilities, Siavash keeps his heart and the doors to this beautiful temple of effort open, willing, and prepared to lend a loving hand. I am proud and honored to be a long-standing member and part of this blossoming community that Siavash has singlehandedly built and fostered. I cannot imagine a life without this gym, or his friendship, and I am forever grateful for the gift of health.

At SixPax Gym, we don't work out—we train.

Gautam Shenoy (before and after)

CHAPTER 14

CARDIO

Many gym classes out there are nothing more than cardio sessions. The intensity is low, and it is impossible to build any significant amount of muscle with them. That doesn't mean cardio is bad! I love doing cardio. As a matter of fact, I usually do 30 to 45 minutes of cardio every day after training.

Cardio is an important part of the equation. You can't get into great shape only by lifting weights. Nutrition is also part of the equation.

There are many benefits to cardio, including:

- → Burning body fat and calories for weight loss
- → Making your heart strong so it doesn't have to work as hard to pump blood
- → Increasing your lung capacity
- → Reducing your risk of heart attack, high cholesterol, high blood pressure, diabetes, and some forms of cancer

→ Making you feel good, and even providing some relief from depression and anxiety

→ Helping you sleep better

→ Helping reduce stress

→ Improving your sex life

→ Giving you more confidence in how you look and feel

→ Increasing bone density if you do weight-bearing cardio exercises

I know some people hate doing cardio. If that's the case, you can join one of those classes to help you get it done in a way that you enjoy. Cardio classes have their place, but don't treat them like training sessions.

Encourage your clients to do some form of cardio, whether that's putting on their headphones while they use the elliptical for 30 minutes, going for a run, or taking a dance class. Stay on them about it and help them to learn why cardio is important and how it should fit into their training routine.

If your clients are new to working out, ask them to walk for 30 to 45 minutes a day to create the habit. Then slowly ask them to make it more intense. Remember, cardio kicks up your metabolism, so your goal is to make it a daily habit for them.

I also like to recommend my clients do their cardio right after training or have a set time they do it so it becomes a daily routine.

Clients often ask me if they should do cardio in the morning on an empty stomach or during the evening. It doesn't matter as long as they do it on a daily basis.

CHAPTER 15

WHAT MAKES MY SIXPAX METHOD UNIQUE

Old-school gyms are basic. Intention and intensity are far more important than fancy equipment and complicated training programs. That means your focus is on compound movements. It's easier to lift heavier weights doing compound exercises such as squats, barbell curls, and shoulder presses, than it is doing isolated ones such as preacher curls. So, I had to be creative.

I created a system inspired by Temple Gym, which is known as the pre-exhausting system. For example, with this system you do two sets of push-ups with 20 reps then try a bench press.

There are many benefits to this system, especially for beginners, including:

→ You won't be able to go too heavy

→ It prevents injuries

→ Having blood in in your muscles already promotes better mind and muscle connection

→ The pump feels amazing

In the early days of SixPax, because of the lack of equipment, I couldn't train people for a standard hour session. I had to reduce it to 30 minutes. But this wasn't a class where people used light weights. This was all-out war with iron for 30 minutes!

In the beginning, I worried we wouldn't be able to fit everything in before time ran out, but new clients couldn't take more than 10 or 15 minutes of the training. I was making a name for myself for being intense! My success came not just from being intense, but from being the right kind of intense.

I pushed people on their limits every day they came to train. I wanted them to leave feeling spent, like they came, gave it their all, and left a winner. I never wanted my clients to leave feeling like a failure. For many trainers, that's a huge mistake. They push clients too hard and don't notice the emotional roller coaster clients are experiencing. Missing that last rep can affect the clients in a big way, so trainers must pay attention to that.

To do this well, you must be vigilant and watch your client closely.

As I said earlier, don't look at your phone when training a client. Ever. It's the fastest way to lose a client and kill your business.

You want to see if a muscle is about to fail or the client's form starts to look a little shaky. If you can tell the client is starting to get tired, give them a few more reps or spot the client to finish the set, let them get that last rep by themselves, and you will see the joy in their face.

CHAPTER 16

TRAINING TIPS

A thousand different experts on training will give you a thousand different theories on how to train the right way. Don't be discouraged if you see other trainers in your area doing things differently.

While there is nothing even approaching agreement on the subject, here are my truths when it comes to training:

Fact #1

To gain muscle and strength, you must give your body a reason to repair and grow. Using heavy loads forces your central nervous system to tell your muscles to fire and recruit as many muscle fibers as possible. Through the principle of progressive overload, you will be adding weight and/or reps each time you perform an exercise. This will help ensure your muscles have to continue adapting and growing to the stress you place them under.

Fact #2

Many different systems will get you the results you're looking for. I've tried all kinds of systems, from volume training to high intensity interval training (HIIT) to Doggcrapp to FST-7—you name it, I've tried it. As long as you're training intensely, you will get results!

In my experience I've found that if people are looking to lose weight and gain muscle, HIIT is the way to go. HIIT is characterized by alternating short, intense exercises with short recovery sessions. It's all about maximum effort in minimal time. Most people can't and don't want to train for many hours at a time, so HIIT is the perfect solution.

Back in the day, bodybuilders were encouraged to train for extended periods of time. I was out of fuel by the end of the session, and there was no way I could do anything but sit and rest for a few hours after that. That is not practical for regular people with normal jobs. Even if you love bodybuilding, training that intense is only doable for a period of time.

To ensure maximum efficiency, I recommend you split your clients' training sessions to focus on different parts of the body. For example, on Mondays you can schedule chest, back, and biceps, and on Thursdays you can schedule legs, shoulders, and triceps.

This helps your clients to know what's coming and prepare for it.

Keeping sessions to only 30 minutes helps your clients to maintain the intensity for the entire session. Many people like to do workouts that are fun, quick, and varied. To keep sessions short, I recommend having your clients do a good warm-up, having fewer sets, and encouraging your clients to go all out.

Keeping your sessions short is good for business, too. Because the sessions were only 30 minutes, I began to attract more successful professionals who had financial resources but minimal time. The 30-minute sessions became our signature and our recipe for success. Even the busiest CEO can find 30 minutes to keep in shape.

CERTIFICATIONS ARE NOT ENOUGH!

There's more to being a good trainer than simply having the right certifications. You have to be able to make people feel comfortable in your space, too. Here are some tried-and-true tips I've found helpful over the years.

Always look your client in the eye and make eye contact. This will help make them feel like you are watching what they're doing and they are safe in your hands. But don't stare at them for more than a few seconds. People will get uncomfortable with that.

Walk around constantly, rotate, and check in with all your clients from different angles. Pay attention to their form. If they need correction, shout out their name and tell them to correct it. Clients love to know you are really paying attention to them and helping them be successful.

Be present. This may sound like a given with the advice I gave above, but I've seen so many trainers distracted by their phones while training clients. They are either on social media or chatting with someone. Even worse, I've seen some trainers shame their clients for wanting their full attention. Clients are more motivated when they know you are involved.

TRAINING WOMEN

Many women are afraid to lift weights because they think they will get bulky and too muscular. You have to educate them on the subject.

Make sure they understand that building muscle is hard, but it also prevents injuries.

To encourage women to be excited about lifting weights, make sure to post a lot of pictures of women who are training at your gym and benefiting from the results. Be sure to ask their permission first. Get their testimonials and post them on social media.

I had a client named Joyce. She was a very smart woman, a medical student working to become a doctor. When she first came to the gym, she couldn't even lift five pounds. She weighed about 100 pounds. She joined the gym at first because she wanted to lose weight.

I spent about 30 minutes talking to her about the benefits of muscle, but she wasn't yet sold on the idea. I trained her three times a week. I thought she would quit! But she was there every session. She started to push herself to lift heavier and noticed changes she liked. Soon, she was standing upright—no more hunching. Her clothes fit better. She got stronger, and she had more energy. The biggest win in my opinion was that she started to believe in herself and her own strength. She is now in love with training!

Be Punctual

You must be punctual—not even a minute late to training! No excuses.

My training sessions start on the dot—not a minute early or late. You set the tone for other trainers. If you or any of your trainers are even five minutes late to class, make that session free for your clients. Every minute counts because the clients are paying for it. This is a sign of respect for them.

CHAPTER 17

NUTRITION

Growing up, I was probably one of the skinniest guys in my school. I was fast, but I wasn't strong. When I competed in taekwondo at 15, I weighed about 122 pounds. Even my mom would make fun of me. She'd tell me she didn't know how my skinny neck could hold up my big head.

I remember lifting weights in the back of the wrestling gym with a bar and a couple of plates and a pull up bar. It was set up so that Olympic wrestlers could train and get stronger. Once, I tried to bench press the 45-pound bar, but I couldn't get it off my chest. One of the wrestlers came and helped me lift the bar off my chest, but not before making fun of me. He said I was training my bones because I had no muscles.

That hurt at the time, but I knew it didn't matter what anyone else said. I wanted to be a bodybuilder. But being a bodybuilder in the town I grew up in was nearly impossible, especially with the food shortages.

When I left Iran, I was 19 years old, and I weighed 160 pounds. At university, I could only afford to buy one meal a day, so I ate that plus the meal the university provided at lunch. I trained hard, but to be a top contender I knew I had to eat a lot of meat and other foods. At that time, I couldn't afford meat. Instead, I ate a lot of rice and bread. I was getting stronger thanks to all the lifting, but I didn't see any muscle separation or many gains.

Once I started training at Temple Gym and learning about Dorian's approach, I realized how important it was to have a good diet, but I still made some mistakes along the way.

I tried to get big—or as bodybuilders call it, bulking. But this was a huge mistake for me. The idea behind bulking is to gain more muscle by consuming a lot of calories, gaining weight, and leaning back out—losing the fat and keeping the additional muscle. Unfortunately, most of those gains come from fat. This was made worse when I didn't pay attention to the quality of food I was eating, so most of the gains I made were fat and water. When I tried to lean back out by dieting down, I lost nearly all the weight I gained and didn't have any more muscle to show for it. It ended up being a waste of time, effort, and money.

I learned it was better to stay close to top shape all year round. You can only gain so much muscle in a year. You can't shortcut the process. I still see many other new bodybuilders making that same mistake as they try to imitate top professionals.

After spending a year in a maximum-security prison, I came out with no muscles. I wasn't allowed outside, and I didn't have anything to train with. I did push-ups and sit-ups in my cell, but that was it. I was given such little food that I lost muscle fast. Some inmates had money and were able to order chips, candy, or chocolate. I didn't have any money, and other inmates weren't allowed to share. I often went hungry and drank water to kill the hunger pains. When I finally got out, I was back to being skinny!

During my journey to turn bodybuilding from a dream into a reality, I hired a nutritionist to help me get ready for competitions. His name was Dave Palumbo. A former bodybuilder and founder of RXmuscle.com, he had a reputation for helping other bodybuilders get ready for shows. Working with him was an eye-opener. I learned so much about fat loss during my 16 weeks of preparation. While working with him, my body fat was less than 7 percent, and I was all veins and muscle! During that 16-week span, I ate zero carbs and did a huge amount of cardio. The results were amazing.

I worked with other nutritionists over the years too. Some methods were extremely complicated and not at all practical, but those nutritionists said their way would give me an edge. Back then it was my goal to bring my body fat down to less than 6 percent and maintain as much muscle as possible. Sometimes that meant eating 10 meals a day. Sometimes it meant eating 30 egg whites a day.

It became a full-time job. For years, I cooked for myself every single day. I calculated every penny I had, and I never ate out. I measured every ounce of meat I ate and logged everything, even my lifts, because that's what Dorian did.

After studying all of the pro-bodybuilders for years and following everything they did in hopes of joining their ranks, I learned a harsh truth: for most of them, illegal steroids were a huge part of the equation. Eventually I had to come to terms with the fact that the risk of doing what it would take to join the best of the best was much higher than the reward.

There are so many myths around steroids. Many people think steroids are the answer to bigger muscles, but they're not a healthy one. Once you start lifting and seeing progress, it's inevitable to want faster results. However, there are many problems associated with taking steroids, including:

→ They are illegal, and by using them you are risking jail time. Simple possession of anabolic steroids carries a maximum penalty of one year in prison and a minimum $1,000 fine if it is an individual's first drug offense. The maximum penalty for trafficking is five years in prison and a fine of $250,000 if this is the individual's first felony drug offense.

→ In men, steroids will shut down natural testosterone production, which will make it difficult to have children.

→ Most steroids are homemade, so you don't really know what you're getting, and that makes them very dangerous.

I have seen so many friends take steroids with the intention of improving their physique and ending up a full-blown drug dealer, sacrificing health, losing a kidney, suffering heart attacks, and dying young. You and your clients can build a beautiful physique with a proper training and nutrition plan.

Everything I learned working with nutritionists was very valuable. When I started training people, I gave them a simple food plan. I made sure it was easy to follow while having a life outside of the gym. Most of my clients had a job and a family. They wanted to look good, sure, but there was no way they were going to follow a bodybuilding regiment.

The meal plan I created included five meals: breakfast, lunch, dinner, and two protein shakes in between. This ensured my clients were getting enough protein to maintain their muscles while they were restricting their calories.

I tell my clients not to worry about counting calories and logging what they eat. It's not practical. Would they count calories for the rest of their lives?

No. I'd rather not make them do something they would stop as soon as they stopped training at SixPax.

Here are a few simple tips on diet I recommend you pass on to your clients:

- → Cut out all junk food and soda from your diet

- → Cut most carbs

- → Push carb meals to breakfast and mid-morning snack

- → Add some healthy fat for dinner

- → Cut calories

You don't have to spend hundreds of dollars on diet products. They often have little to no value that you can't get with food.

Here's a simple example of a basic food plan I might recommend to a client:

Meal 1: Two to three whole organic eggs, plus either one cup of cooked oats or two pieces of toast and blueberries

Meal 2: Protein shake

Meal 3: Four to six ounces of turkey, beef, chicken, or any kind of protein plus one cup of veggies and a half cup of rice or pasta

Meal 4: Protein shake plus one spoonful of peanut butter or almond butter

Meal 5: Four to six ounces of turkey, beef, chicken, or red meat plus a cup of veggies and a handful of almonds

SAMPLE SHOPPING LIST

Here's a sample of a basic shopping list you can pass along to your clients to make sure you cover all the dieting necessities: Personally, I always try to buy as much as I can fresh and/or in bulk.

Not all of these items are required, but it's a good list to work from.

Protein Sources

- ☑ Boneless, skinless chicken breast. Buy the organic type—it's a couple dollars more, but it is absolutely worth it. It tastes so much better.
- ☑ Top round steak
- ☑ Flank steak
- ☑ Eye of round steak
- ☑ Protein powder (whey, casein, egg)
- ☑ Fish (salmon, tuna, tilapia, cod)
- ☑ Fresh eggs—I love eggs!

Carbohydrate Sources

- ☑ Old-fashioned oats
- ☑ Rice (brown, white, basmati)
- ☑ Sweet potatoes
- ☑ Red skin potatoes

☑ Baked potatoes

☑ Wheat bread

Fat Sources

☑ All-natural peanut butter

☑ Extra virgin olive oil

☑ Fish oil capsules

☑ Almonds

☑ Walnuts

☑ Cashews

☑ Flaxseed oil

☑ Coconut oil

☑ Avocado

Vegetable Sources

☑ Broccoli

☑ Cauliflower

☑ Asparagus

☑ Cucumbers

☑ Pickles

☑ Celery

- ☑ Spinach
- ☑ Mushrooms
- ☑ Green salads

Condiments and Spices

- ☑ Salt
- ☑ Pepper
- ☑ Mrs. Dash seasonings
- ☑ Cinnamon
- ☑ Soy sauce
- ☑ Salsa
- ☑ Hot sauce
- ☑ Dijon mustard

SHOPPING TIPS

I recommend you buy in bulk. Do your grocery shopping at a warehouse grocer such as Costco.

I like to start off my mornings with a blended shake consisting of dry oats, egg whites, and a healthy fat like coconut oil.

If you are not a fan of egg whites, you can use protein powder. All you'll have to do is put it in the blender with a little water or low-calorie almond milk, and blend it for a minute. This way you will have no excuses to skip this meal.

Prepare all your meals on one day of the week. Choose a day when you're not very busy, like Sunday, to cook all your meats, vegetables, and other foods. Divide what you prepare into meals in separate containers. Then, each night before you go to bed, take out what you need for the next day.

Or you can simply order meals from a meal prep company—this has saved me tons of money and time. Do your research and find someone who delivers fresh, healthy, and affordable meals.

LOW-CARB DIET

If you want to get in shape, keep it simple and practical. I have seen so many people start off with fancy diet plans, only to get burned out, stop, and lose all their progress. This cycle can repeat on and off for years without making a real difference if the plan is too complicated.

If you want to lose body fat, you must reduce your carb intake. Please do not argue about this! So, knowing that, the recipe for success is simple: Reduce your carbs, add some cardio, and keep training hard at the gym. Nothing fancy, and no headache of calculating and monitoring.

Can you still get into shape while eating carbs? Yes, absolutely. You just have to pay closer attention to your diet. But why would you want to do that when you already have so many things to think about every day?

Personally, I've learned to systemize everything so I can do it without thinking. I just follow the process and get the job done. It makes everything a lot easier. But it's important to remember, that no matter what, dieting isn't easy. You might as well make it simple.

KETO DIET

I'm a big fan of the keto diet. Back in 2009 when I was getting ready for my first competition at a bodybuilding show, my nutritionist Dave Palumbo, taught me a lot about my diet. Before working with him, I was always in bulk mode. I ate as much as I could to gain muscle, but I also gained fat.

I spent a lot of time researching how to gain muscle, how to tax muscle, and how to increase my intensity without getting injured. But I hadn't learned much about dieting at that point.

Palumbo was a big fan of keto, so I started the zero-carb diet. It lasted for four months, with me taking a break every two weeks for a cheat meal. For my cheat meal, I usually ate a burger and fries. I loved keto because I didn't have any cravings or mood swings when I was losing body fat. I did tons of cardio as well, losing one to three pounds a week, which was ideal.

So, on top of keto, I was doing more than an hour of cardio a day to train. By the end of it, I had less than 6 percent body fat, and I looked amazing.

Back in the day, I was willing to try all kinds of diets to give me a chance to become a professional bodybuilder. I would have even tried eating dog poop to reach my goal—but thankfully it didn't come to that!

Keto works, but it's not practical for most people and can be difficult to maintain in the long-term. To do it right, you must avoid all carbs at all costs to stay in ketosis, otherwise you have to start all over again. If you cheat a couple of times a week, your progress slows down, and you lose motivation.

So, what's the answer here? Let me explain a few things before we get into some more detail.

All human beings have bodies that function similarly. But as much as we're alike, there are also many differences between us. What's important here are these two factors: genetics and environment.

You can look and feel great if you understand how to manipulate these two factors.

GENETICS

Genetics impact the way you look. They also impact your unique biochemistry—specifically hormones, the chemical messengers in your body that govern all of its processes.

For example, my right-hand man, Peri, could eat a horse and never gain a pound. Sometimes his metabolism kicks up and he even loses weight. I feel bad for him because I see him eating so much in an effort to gain a few pounds. Yet there are others out there who would love to have this problem.

Some well-known hormones include:

- → Insulin

- → Glucagon

- → Thyroid hormones

- → Growth hormones

- → Testosterone

- → Estrogen

All of these hormones have very powerful effects on the body. Manipulate any of them and you will notice results almost immediately. Many, if not

SMALL GYM BIG RESULTS

all hormones are at least indirectly (if not directly) related to your diet, and consequently impact how you feel, look, function, and perform.

ENVIRONMENT

When I talk about environment here, I'm talking about where you live, but more importantly what you do to your body—how you eat and how you take care of yourself, which includes exercise and rest. In bodybuilding, we try to control as much as we can.

Why I Believe in the Power of Low-Carb Diets

I have trained thousands of people. I've tried many different diets. The one I found most effective was the simple and practical low-carb diet.

Low carb diets have been around for ages. Our hunter-gatherer ancestors only consumed fiber (from vegetables, fruits, and tubers) as a carbohydrate source. If you don't eat carbs for the rest of your life, nothing will happen to you. You will survive. But if you cut something like fat out of your diet, you will have all kinds of issues!

Humans didn't start consuming carbohydrates in large quantities until the development of agriculture, around 10,000 years ago[5]—relatively recently, in the timeline of human history. Nowadays, nearly every meal we eat has carbohydrates, and much of it is refined.

In the 1970s, Dr. Robert Atkins popularized the low-carb approach for losing weight (and gaining health). I believe this is a very practical way of dieting for most people.

WHO SHOULD USE THIS DIET?

Typically, people with a slower metabolism should follow a low-carb diet. If you gain weight easily, a low-carb approach will probably help you. If you find you don't handle carbs the same way you did when you were younger, you might want to give this diet a try. It works great for men and women alike.

THE BASICS

The main premise of the low-carb approach is that by keeping carbohydrate consumption low, the body is more efficient at fat burning, as fat can't be burned in the presence of insulin. The body switches over to using fat for fuel rather than carbohydrates in a process known as ketosis.

However, ketosis isn't necessarily required for a successful low-carb diet. You can make great progress even when you are not in ketosis.

How? Well, keeping insulin levels low helps to regulate your appetite and keeps you feeling better. Without carbs in your diet, you don't have the ups and downs of blood sugar regulations, the consequences of hormonal hunger, or the tired, worn-down feeling following a carb-heavy meal. The hormone glucagon, which is released when blood glucose levels get too low, acts opposite to insulin. Glucagon releases fat from the fat cells to be used as fuel by the body.

SETTING UP THE VERY LOW-CARB DIET

There are many variations of this kind of diet available, but the one I will present here is typically higher in protein than most. This will help to maintain muscle, and you can keep your heavy training. It also focuses more on healthy fats.

Here is the basic daily setup:

Daily protein needed in grams   =   (lean body mass in pounds) X 1

Daily good fat needed in grams   =   (lean body mass in pounds) X 0.5

Using the table above, a 200-pound male at 20 percent body fat (160 pounds lean body mass) would follow a plan like this:

Protein = 160 X 1 for 160 grams per day

Fat = 160 X 0.5 for 80 grams per day

Dividing this across five meals equates to 32 grams of protein and roughly 16 grams of fat per meal. If you prefer eating six meals per day, divide the total by six.

A 150-pound female with 25 percent body fat (113 pounds lean body mass) would follow a plan like this:

Protein = 113 X 1 for 113 grams of protein per day

Fat = 113 X 0.5 for 57 grams of fat per day

Divide this by five meals to get 23 grams of protein and roughly 10 grams of fat. Again, if you prefer eating six meals per day, just divide the total by six.

For protein, you should focus on high quality, low carb sources such as chicken, fish, beef, eggs, and protein powder such as whey isolate.

Do your research and find a good protein powder. When I look for a good protein powder, I always look at the ingredients. Whey isolate must be the first ingredient, and I'm checking for high numbers in protein and low amounts of carbs and fat.

For the fats, focus on healthy ones such as extra virgin olive oil, macadamia nut oil, all-natural peanut butter, almonds, walnuts, cashews, and pecans.

That can be a lot for clients to take in. They might feel overwhelmed, especially in the beginning. Dieting can be rough, even when you've done it before and you know how to handle it. So how can you help your clients get on track?

→ Keep it simple. Counting calories or counting macros is not practical in my opinion, and people won't stick to the diet. Keep the instructions simple to help clients understand what makes food healthy and what doesn't. If you can't grow it, pick it, or kill it, it's probably too processed.

→ As clients get used to eating healthier food, have them eat smaller meals throughout the day, three to four hours apart.

→ Encourage your clients to meal prep or use a meal prep company so they don't have to worry about shopping, cooking, and washing dishes.

→ Have your clients start their mornings with two to three eggs and oats. I like to use dry oats, egg whites, and berries. I like to mix them all together and make pancakes.

→ Encourage your clients to keep a case of protein drinks in their car in case they have to work late or get stuck somewhere. This can help them stay on track when they are busy and have no access to healthy food. You can stock up on bottled water, nuts, and protein shakes.

→ When I crave something sweet, I drink tea or Crystal Light. There are a lot of zero calorie snacks out there, so let your clients do their research and find something they like.

→ Encourage your clients to stick to water, diet soda, black coffee, or tea, sweetened with calorie-free sweetener if necessary.

→ Use calorie-free condiments and spices.

→ Use calorie-free sweeteners such as Splenda, Stevia, or Equal.

CHAPTER 18

TALK ABOUT OTHER HEALTH BENEFITS

Bodybuilding is obviously a way for clients to begin to look better and build muscle, but that's not the only reason exercise is important. Weight management and consistent exercise programs have so many other health benefits. It's important to talk about those with your clients, too.

DISEASE PREVENTION

Many diseases have been linked to a poor diet and a lack of exercise, such as heart disease. Heart disease is the number one leading cause of death in both men and women in the United States.[6] Heart disease can take different forms, but the most common type in the U.S. is coronary artery disease, which can lead to a heart attack.[7]

The foods you choose to eat can strongly influence your heart health, so changing your diet can greatly reduce your risk of heart disease.

One recent scientific study suggested that about one-third of cancer deaths could be prevented with changes in lifestyle from diet to exercise.[8]

For Americans who don't use tobacco, which is an entirely different can of worms, dietary choices and physical activity are the most important and controllable of the cancer risk factors.

Beyond that, more than two-thirds of American adults are overweight or obese.[9] That impacts more than just how people look. Obesity is linked to more than 60 chronic diseases, including type 2 diabetes, heart disease, stroke, and more.[10]

HOW TO HELP CLIENTS WHO CAN'T (FOR WHATEVER REASON) FOLLOW YOUR NUTRITION PLAN

Sometimes, while working with clients, you run into complicated situations. Maybe they have a hormonal issue or allergy, or your approach simply isn't a good fit for them. You can and should refer clients to weight management programs that will work for their specific needs. These programs should teach them how to eat healthier based on their circumstances and develop healthy, lifelong habits.

Remember, we're not doctors, and we have limitations. Simply explain to your client that you don't feel comfortable giving nutrition advice and refer them to someone who has more experience and expertise with those issues. Your clients will appreciate your honesty and care.

IMPROVED QUALITY OF LIFE

When you eat healthy and move your body well, your quality of life improves. You have more strength and stamina to ride your bike, hike a mountain, or go swimming with your children. We all want a good quality of life. Without it, we're missing out on years where we can be healthy and enjoy having a healthy body. This can be a great motivator for clients who are looking to make healthy, long-term changes in their lives.

Client Testimonial: *Errol David*

My name is Eroll David, and I am one of the main coaches at SixPax. I still get trained by Siavash two times a week, and that's really where it all began.

I fell in love with fitness in my 20s and wished I could become a personal trainer. I wanted to get into a classic physique competition and planned to after I finished cooking school.

But I gave up on my fitness goals for a long time after a back injury I got from lifting heavy weights with improper form. Fear pushed me away from my passion, and I chose to follow the money in my early career.

I became a truck driver of an 18-wheeler and drove across the country nearly twice a year.

Unfortunately, the money was bad, and the pandemic crisis changed my luck for the worse. I went into a really bad season and was depressed and jobless for some time.

Then I came across SixPax Gym. I decided to make a commitment to train the proper and safe way with a proper nutrition plan, following the SixPax Gym system. Beyond that, I wanted to help train others.

When I met Siavash, I told him about my goals and my dreams. He told me, "You are still young, and you can still do it. It's not too late, but you need to learn and gain experience."

My life changed after hearing those words. Siavash shed some light on me and the dark path I was trying to recover from. He helped give me the confidence and motivation I needed. Training-wise, he pushed me and my body to the limit until I lost the extra weight. I'm now in the best shape of my life. This pushed me to get certified as a professional trainer and nutrition coach.

SixPax Gym is so special to me. It didn't only change my body—it changed my life, inside and out. Now, my dream of being a personal trainer has come true, and Siavash has given me the opportunity to grow here and gain the knowledge I need to be at the top of my game as a personal trainer. I also have the chance to help inspire new warriors to get into the best shape of their lives.

I'm having the best time of my life while training other new warriors and giving them the guidance they need because I've been there before. I know it's completely possible to achieve their body goals, whether that's gaining weight or losing weight. My dream is to own a SixPax Gym of my own someday.

I know that if you put in the work and follow the SixPax system, it works. It changed my life. It can change yours too.

Erroll David (before and after)

PART THREE
Run

CHAPTER 19

WHAT IS YOUR STORY?

Who are you? What is your story? Why did you open your gym? How did you open your gym? You'll need to have an answer for all of these questions, because people will ask them all the time!

As the leader of a gym, you must have a story that shows your struggle, your vision, your dreams, and your mistakes. A good story will catch people's attention and make them want to root for you. They will want to see you win. They'll want to contribute to your gym and what you stand for.

Make a shit list of all the unpleasant stuff you've been through and all the hard times you've experienced. Don't be ashamed of your experiences. Write everything down and what kind of lesson you learned from it. Anything on that list is part of what made you the man or woman who you are today.

Then write down your goal. What do you want your legacy to be?

It might take you awhile to write a good story. That's okay. Keep writing and polishing it up! Share it with as many people as you can and take in their feedback. The more you share your story and repeat it, the better you'll get at telling it. This story will become an important element as you begin to lead your movement.

As you write your story, make sure you are living it. Act professionally. Look people in the eye. Keep your word. Give firm handshakes. Acknowledge people when they walk into your gym.

I have seen so many of my "heroes" and walked away disappointed because they weren't their story. Sometimes they turn into jerks because they forget about their humble beginnings and all the attention goes to their heads. Sometimes they are in the industry just to make a name for themselves and don't really care that much about their clients. Sometimes it's because they are insecure.

Whatever the reason, it's disappointing—but you get to be the hero in this story. You just have to live it out, keep your ego in check, your feet on the ground, and remember where you came from.

Do not try to make up fake stories, because you will forget what you said, and it doesn't look good if your story constantly changes. Adding or exaggerating struggles won't help you in the long run. Be real, be YOU! The foundation of a solid business is honesty.

CHAPTER 20

PAYMENTS AND PRICING

> 66 *There are two kinds of companies, those that work to try to charge more and those that work to charge less.*[11]
>
> —JEFF BEZOS

Many trainers look around and copy others when it comes to pricing. They often start to price themselves lower than everyone else to build some reputation then plan to work their way up.

That's what I did at first! But there's a problem with that. If you copy other trainers, you let their bad systems impact you. Most of them aren't making serious money.

DO YOUR RESEARCH

A big part of pricing is location. If your gym is in Beverly Hills, you can charge a lot more, not only because you're in a high-income community, but because your rent and taxes are impacted by your location too. You'll need to charge more to keep the doors open.

Go back to your dream client list. What is most important to you?

I could, for example, charge twice as much as I charge now and still have clients, but my marketing strategy would have to change. Many clients will join because they want to work with the best, but they won't be able to handle the payments over the long run, so eventually they'll quit. That's bad for retention. And because I love to build community, that wouldn't be a model I want to work with. 70 percent of my clients at SixPax have been training with me for over a year. Many clients have trained with me for more than five years. One of the biggest reasons is my pricing. It's practical. It's not a stretch. But it's not too cheap. Cheap prices will make people suspicious of you. Trainers with high-level skills won't waste their time charging so little.

ASKING FOR PAYMENTS

Many trainers are great at training people and educating clients but are very bad at asking clients to pay. I was one of them! I felt bad, sometimes even rude, asking people for money. Sometimes clients' payments would decline, or they would forget to pay me, and I was uncomfortable bringing it up. Then I'd get angry when I trained them for free!

Once I had a client who I was friendly with. We always had a good time training together, and we talked about fun stuff after our sessions. But he was bad with payments. He would always be a few weeks late, and I felt bad asking him to pay because he was a friend. When I did ask him, he often said he'd pay next time, and then he'd forget again. It got to the point I didn't enjoy training him anymore.

One day I sat him down and told him his payment is what keeps the doors open. I gave him a date to pay and told him if he was late, he wouldn't be able to train until he got that payment in. I made it clear for both of us what we needed to do! It was uncomfortable, but it was important. If you don't confront those issues, they will build up and burn you out. Thankfully, he understood where I was coming from and made his payments on time after that.

Don't be afraid to ask for money. You deserve every penny. Without it, you won't be able to keep the doors open and you will be doing a greater disservice to your clients. You might have to ask two or three times for the money.

More than likely, your clients are professionals who live busy lives and need to be reminded once in a while. They probably won't be offended if you ask them to pay, and you shouldn't be offended if they forget. Payment is just a necessary part of the process.

To minimize mistakes happening with payments, and to eliminate uncomfortable conversations about money, I recommend having a recurring payment software so the payments are taken automatically. The software I use is called Mindbody. It collects the payments on a monthly schedule, and if a card fails, it emails the client to update their card. That way you don't have to remind clients every time, and they won't have to remember! Mindbody also enables clients to schedule their own sessions. It's not the prettiest software or the easiest to learn as a gym owner, but it's been a big part of my success.

After their free session, when I sign a new client up, I ask for their card on the spot. I tell them all I need from them is their card, which I will put into the software. Then I charge it on their first day. That's it! And it continues to charge that client every month that they continue at SixPax. That might sound simple. And it is.

DECLINED PAYMENTS AND REFUNDS

I once signed up a client and made a commitment to get him in shape. I wrote him a good plan, and I started training him. I followed up with him every day and checked in on his progress. After two weeks, he had lost seven pounds! And then he asked me for a refund. He told me he had decided to do something else.

I was so frustrated and angry. I put so much time into this client. He even got results. And still, he wanted to stop the program!

I had two choices. I could either get into an ugly conversation with him and not give him a refund, or I could give the money back. I knew if I chose the first route, it would ruin my day and have an effect on the other great clients I was training that day.

So, I didn't say a word. I just refunded him with a smile on my face. I thanked him for training with us and sent him on his way.

I was a boiling pot on the inside that day, but I did the right thing. The funny thing is, a year after he asked for a refund, he returned to the gym. He *and* his girlfriend trained with me for six months to get in shape for their wedding. I am so happy I gave him a refund.

Giving out refunds used to eat at me for days. It felt personal, but it wasn't. And that's an important lesson for you to learn.

If a client asks for a refund, don't take it personally! Take a step back, calm down, and look into the problem.

Hear them out. Listen to what they have to say and learn from the feedback they give you. Don't get defensive. It can be uncomfortable, but if you act professionally and learn from the complaint, you can make your gym even better.

And finally, if someone asks for a refund, give it to them, and let it go. Whatever the amount of the refund is, it's worth far less than the damage they can cause online with a bad review. Plus, the customer can always get their money back from their bank by filing a chargeback. And when you get a chargeback, not only do you lose the money, but you also get fined. And if you get too many chargebacks, you can lose your ability to take credit card payments ever again.

So the moral to this story is: if someone asks for a refund GIVE IT TO THEM! It will save you money and stress, and most importantly, it will protect your reputation.

If you deal with credit cards, and if you follow my advice and set up recurring payments so you make money while you sleep, you will eventually run into issues with a client's card declining at some point.

You want to make sure those payments go through. The Mindbody software sends a notification to the client when their card declines and prompts them to update their card. Clients usually update it right away, but if they don't, reach out to them immediately. Either call, text, or email them to let them know about the problem.

Example:

Good morning _____,

Hope you are doing well. For some reason your credit card was declined. You may update it online or please bring your new card and
we can update it for you at the gym. Thanks and have a great day.

Siavash @sixpax_gym

Give them the benefit of the doubt here. It might just be because of a tech-
nical issue, or their card expired. Sometimes it might be because a client
can't afford to pay at that time. A declined payment is more likely about
them and what's going on in their life than it is about you.

YOUR OFFER

I have seen so many different offers from different gyms. When I worked
with marketing agencies, they would create a juicy offer, like a six-week
challenge or one week of free access to the gym to bring in new prospects,
but those gimmicks never worked for me. My goal was to just get potential
clients to show up and try my training session once, and I give them so
much value they can't refuse. It also gets them in the mindset that they have
nothing to lose when they try your gym.

I have tried so many different offers, but my favorite is giving away one free
session. It's as simple as it gets.

It's the business model of a drug dealer letting you try the product for free
and then you get hooked. I just want them to try that first free session, and
I have no doubt they will have such a good experience that even if they
don't sign up the same day, they will return at some point.

Your main focus should be getting them to try your gym once. You can get creative with this by offering free body fat testing, a free T-shirt, or anything that encourages them to take the first step. For most people, the first step is the hardest.

CHARGE PER SESSION OR PACKAGE

Many trainers charge per session. Clients pay you for 10 or 20 sessions, or they may even buy single sessions at a time. This is a disaster! How do I know this? This is exactly how I started out, and it wasn't worth it.

Charging money up front means your income is unpredictable and most people can't afford it.

I used to charge $600 for 12 sessions or $1,500 for 36 sessions. It felt awesome to collect that big check, but that money soon disappeared. I spent it on rent, new equipment, or other expenses, but I still owed the client another three months of training—and that's if they didn't take any breaks.

If something came up, like a vacation or they got sick, their next payment could be months away.

I couldn't predict my income. Some months I made $10,000. Some months I made nothing. One day I checked my bank account and realized I was nearly broke—but I owed 360 sessions to my clients!

That was a wake-up call for me. That system didn't work, and I needed to figure out a different one.

Charge a Monthly Subscription

Bingo!

This is my favorite method. I've found that if people pay up front for big packages, they can lose steam and feel like they are being held hostage if they can't back out. With a monthly subscription, clients are free to leave and join whenever they want to. This helps to make the process as simple as possible. Fake gurus advise against this because they are worried about retention, but in my experience, this method actually helps with retention. You will end up growing a culture, not just the number of clients. This system will weed out the people who are not committed and will nurture the good clients by being flexible.

Plus, when you give your client some flexibility, they know you care about them beyond just the money they give you.

Money is fuel for us to push the movement and help more people, and it is important for you to have predictable income—but your clients need to know that you understand they are people with their own lives, too. If they get sick or something unexpected comes up, having some flexibility with them will go a long way.

Serving 279 clients at $299 per month will equal $1 million a year. It's a win-win situation. The clients are happy, and you are going to have an amazing life just like me!

Semi-Private Classes

I did one-on-one training sessions for many years when I started the gym, but I eventually learned that one-on-one training was not scalable. My business would never grow because there was only one of me. I've found semi-private classes work best. This allows you to serve more clients, charge them less, and make more money.

When I first pivoted to semi-private, I trained three people at a time by myself. To scale even more, I added an assistant coach. Currently at SixPax, there are never more than six people in a session, and there are always two trainers present—one head coach and one assistant coach.

I've also found that having a small group helps to motivate your clients to do their best, even if they come in after a long day of work. Seeing others go hard motivates everyone! The more clients come in at the same time and train together, the more they get to know each other and become friends. That's a big part of how you build a real community.

Working with groups is also more fun for the trainers.

You can still post your one-on-one prices on your website. This will show the huge price difference to your clients and help them understand they can get results at a good value with semi-private training.

With this setup, clients are either training up to eight sessions a month (twice a week) or up to 12 sessions a month (three times a week). The sessions do not roll over to the next month.

After clients try a free session, I usually recommend they start training twice a week to build their foundation. I explain to them the importance of healthy eating and following a food plan. I give them a cardio regimen of 30 to 45 minutes a day to get maximum results.

Joining the SixPax Gym includes training with a professional trainer, a practical food plan, a SixPax t-shirt, body fat testing, and access to the gym seven days a week to do cardio.

We over-deliver on value, and we help them as much as we can.

Some months, for example, are longer than others, and clients may run out of sessions and ask for their billing cycle to be changed to an earlier date so they can keep up with training two to three times a week. We have a single session purchase option, but instead of charging it, I usually honor the extra session to reward them for being consistent and engaged. They appreciate this, and it helps with retention.

WHEN CLIENTS LEAVE

Many clients will eventually reach their goals or just decide to quit training. When they do, make the experience as pleasant as possible. Thank them for training with you and encourage them to keep up the good work.

Usually, I give them a training routine to do on their own and honor any sessions they missed. I tell them it was fun training with them, and I ask them to write a review so I can attract more clients like them. In my experience, this results in clients either coming back to the gym or referring other people to it.

CHAPTER 21

RULES TO PROTECT YOU

It's easy to get swept up in the excitement of finally owning your own gym and bringing in clients. After all, it is exciting! But it's also important to create structures and systems that will protect you as a business owner.

DON'T LET SESSIONS ROLL OVER

This will benefit you by keeping your systems simple, eliminating the need to track what's going on with each membership. Instead, create your system so that subscriptions renew each month. This will also ensure that clients actually show up to their training sessions. At SixPax, this means, clients agree to train either up to eight sessions a month (two times a week) or up to 12 sessions a month (three times a week). The sessions do not roll over to the next month.

Besides making this simpler for you on the back end, it also helps keep clients accountable. If there are no financial consequences to missing your twice a week, 30-minute training sessions, many clients are tempted to slack off. They let themselves go and have a hard time getting in shape. That makes you look bad!

I used to stay on top of them and constantly remind them to show up, but that didn't work. This no-rollover system will help prevent you from getting burned out.

Of course, you will sometimes have clients who complain about the sessions they lost. And maybe they really did have a good excuse.

You should stick to your no-rollover rule for the most part, but don't write it in stone. If a client is upset and demands the session, don't argue with them—just honor the session and move forward. This is a good way to keep client retention a priority while also providing clients incentive to show up. Remember, the SixPax way is all about the small gym with a touch of care. We want clients to win and succeed. Make an exception for them. Tell the client you are proud of them for wanting to push themselves.

24-HOUR CANCELLATION POLICY

A 24-hour cancellation will benefit both you and the client.

I used to allow people to cancel last minute. I really tried to work with them because I know life happens. But at one point I had clients booking themselves eight times only to show up for four of them. There were no consequences.

Clients might decide an hour before their session that they're too tired today and will show up tomorrow instead. But that means I lost two sessions!

The client canceled, and it's too late to have someone else fill that slot.

A 24-hour cancellation policy helps keep clients accountable. If something more important comes up—because things come up in life—clients then have to let you know in time. That way you can reschedule the session and fill that spot with someone else.

This is standard practice for many other businesses, so don't be afraid to enforce this rule. Of course, it's important to be nice and understanding once in a while, because this is a people business, and sometimes real emergencies do happen, but this policy in writing will help to deter flakiness and save you a lot of time and frustration.

CHAPTER 22

SIXPAX TECH SECRETS

SixPax may look and feel like an old-school gym, but below the surface, it's the software we use that drives our growth and keeps us organized and running smoothly. I'm not a high-tech person, and you don't have to be super techy either to use the best programs. In this chapter, I will share with you all my software secrets so you can see how SixPax Gym operates on the back end.

1. Mindbody

This is the most important software we use. I use it to schedule clients, to process recurring monthly payments, issue refunds, and keep track of client progress and history. We also use it to track our revenue and determine how many active clients we have. I share this information with my team on a daily basis. We also use Mindbody to nurture our existing clients with built-in email automation.

2. GoHighLevel

This is our customer relationship management (CRM) software, a sales and marketing follow-up system. We use it to send automated nurture emails to leads. And by connecting it to another software called Twilio, we can also send automated SMS text messages. We use it to send emails and texts to all the new leads who fill out the form on our site to request a free training session.

Here's our lead sequence:

1. Lead fills out form for a free session.

2. They see a thank-you page thanking them and telling them that I will call to schedule a free session.

3. Lead contact info comes to our email and GoHighLevel software. Our entire team is alerted.

4. Immediately we call the lead to schedule them. We try to call them within five minutes.

5. If they answer, we book them for their free session.

6. If they don't answer the call, we send them a text that says, "Thank you for reaching out! Please let me know what day and time you are available so I can schedule your free session thank you. —Siavash from SixPax Gym"

7. If they answer, we book them for their free session.

8. They receive a confirmation of appointment right away.

9. They receive a reminder 24 hours before the appointment.

10.   We text them again on the same day of the appointment with a friendly reminder.

11.   If they don't show up, the system will send them a three-part no-show email sequence to try to get them to schedule their free session.

12.   We also text and call every day for three days, then once a week for the next month to get them to schedule their free session.

This automated nurture system doubled our revenue. It used to take 30 hours a week for us to do this follow-up, and now it's all automated through this software. Plus, we can see exactly where each client is in this process.

3. ClickFunnels

This is a drag-and-drop site builder, designed by and for marketers. Building a website and dealing with a programmer can be a pain in the neck. Save yourself the time and headache and use ClickFunnels for your site. So many web designers have reached out to try to sell me a more beautiful site and design, but we have made millions of dollars using this simple website. Plus, we love the ClickFunnels community. We have learned a lot about marketing and business from them, and we will be loyal customers for years to come.

4. Zapier

Zapier is an online automation tool that connects your apps to create a workflow. Each automation is called a "zap." At SixPax we use Zapier to send information or trigger an action between MindBody, GoHighLevel, Google Sheets, and ClickFunnels.

Here are a few examples:

New Leads (from ads, our site, or walk-ins)
When a new lead fills out a form from a Facebook ad, or on our site, or a landing page in our ClickFunnels, a zap sends that same lead's information to our CRM (GoHighLevel) to start them on a drip email sequence.

Free Session - No Show
When a new lead schedules a free training session and doesn't show up, a zap is sent to our CRM, to start that customer on a new drip email sequence to let them know that we care and to schedule a new session.

Membership Purchase
When a new membership is purchased in Mindbody, a zap is sent to our CRM to update their status and start that customer on a new member drip email sequence.

Customer Information Update
When any customer's information is updated in MindBody, a zap is sent to our CRM to update that information.

Membership Terminated in Mindbody
When membership is terminated in Mindbody, a zap is sent to our CRM to send that customer a confirmation email and tag the customer as terminated.

5. Twilio

We use this software, which is connected to our Mindbody and GoHighLevel software, to send automated messages to clients by SMS text. We make sure all our clients opt in to our text messaging by asking them to sign the waiver when they join the gym. There are strict rules about sending

SMS text messages so be sure to follow your state rule and regulations.

6. SignNow

This cloud-based digital signature software makes it easy for new clients to sign documentation on the spot in our gym. No one, not even friends or family, can train or even touch any equipment at SixPax without first signing our waiver and terms of service on our iPad with SignNow. The software can be used on iPhone, iPad, and Android devices.

7. Google Workspace (Gmail, Docs, Sheets, etc.)

All our important documents are created, organized, and saved on Google Workspace. It's much safer and more secure than storing files on your own computer. Our @SixPaxGym.com company email accounts are also live here. Since everything is stored in the cloud, I can access all our documents from any device wherever I am.

8. Slack (Team Communication)

Our entire SixPax team communicates on Slack, so we all can see and be updated instantly. We can communicate one-on-one or with an entire channel. We have channels for clients, trainers, updates, issues, meetings, and scripts. We also have channels dedicated to quick access to the vendor directory in case there is an emergency.

Here are the names of a few channels we use so everyone on my team can communicate:

- → SixPax Company Mission & Vision (Stored Notes)

→ Exercise Routine (Stored Notes)

→ General (Communication)

→ Lead Follow-up (Communication)

→ Scripts (Stored Notes)

→ SixPax Gym Values (Stored Notes)

→ Team Meeting (Communication)

→ Time-Off Requests (Communication)

→ Vendor Directory (Stored Notes)

10. Asana (Project Management)

We build and track all company projects and tasks here. We can assign them to any team member, and we can all access any project to see what progress has been made. It helps us to organize, track, and manage our work. It's excellent for making sure we are completing not only our day-to-day tasks but future projects and assignments as well.

11. Paychex (Payroll)

There are many payroll companies out there, but my accountant recommended we use Paychex, and we have been using it ever since. We have access to the portal and can get any reports we need.

12. QuickBooks

We use this for bookkeeping and accounting. We can switch accountants or bookkeepers without losing any information. All our data is stored on the cloud, and all are bank accounts are connected to it so my bookkeeper can give me a monthly report.

13. Review Trigger

We use this software to collect reviews. It allows clients to write a review using any platform they like, such as Google, Facebook, Yelp, and more. We simply ask a client if they can write a review so we can attract more committed clients like them. We usually ask them when they share a win with us, we text them with the link, and as soon as they write it, we get a notification as well.

14. Lucidchart

This easy-to-use software helps create organizational charts. We use it to draw charts and to map out our processes.

15. Facebook, Instagram, YouTube (Social Media)

We use these powerful social media platforms for organic marketing and to help us communicate with our potential and existing clients. It allows them to see what we are all about without having to physically be at SixPax. Posting multiple times a day has enabled me to become a local celebrity in my town, with people recognizing me wherever I go. I imagine these social media platforms as my own TV channel, so I try to bring three things to viewers: information, entertainment, and value. We also buy paid ads on these platforms.

16. Music

We use Pandora or Spotify in the gym. We make sure to adjust the settings so there is no foul language, because many clients bring their children. Remember this is a gym, not a club—keep the music for the background. Have fun with the training playlists, but remember not everyone likes rap or rock. Mix it up and keep it fun.

17. Apple

I own an iPhone, and it's very easy to use. I am not very tech savvy, so I like simple stuff. I want everything to be in one place, so my computer and laptop are Apple, too—they are all connected to each other, and it makes my life so much easier. I can have access to all my pictures, documents, and many other things anywhere I am on any of these devices.

18. InBody

This is a pricey tool to measure body fat, but clients love it because they get a printout of their body composition and their info is saved. So, next time we do the test on the InBody machine, we can compare the results. Don't worry about getting this machine right away. For years, I used a hand-held fat loss monitor with my clients. It will still give you a way to measure your clients' progress. When you can afford it, though, an In-Body machine will take your measurements to the next level.

19. Security Cameras

This is a must for every gym. Make sure you have a camera system in place that covers every corner of the gym. You don't want any blind spots! This will protect you against false claims and make people think twice before trying anything. This is a deterrent, so post a huge sign showing that you have cameras. We hired a company to install the cameras, and pay a small monthly fee to maintain them. Our cameras are small and installed in places people can't see, so to further deter people from any funny business, we bought a huge fake camera and put it outside of the gym.

20. Mint

This is a simple app you can download to your phone and connect to all your bank accounts. It's a great way to track your net worth, keep track of your bills and budgets, and set savings goals. I love it because it's simple.

CHAPTER 23

TAXES, PAPERWORK, AND LIABILITY

The last thing you want to do is get into legal trouble because you accidentally made a mistake or did something wrong. Accountants and lawyers can help keep you out of trouble.

A lawyer can also help draft up a waiver that protects you from liability if someone gets hurt or something goes wrong, draft a contract for contractors and employees, help you trademark your name, and so much more.

Do not train anyone under any circumstances without a waiver, not even your best friend. Make them sign a waiver. I use the app SignNow for this. I ask the client to come in 15 minutes before the session so I can weigh them and have them sign the waiver on my iPad before the session starts.

If they act annoyed with this requirement, refuse to train them. Don't feel guilty about making them sign the document. It has nothing to do with trust—it's just part of the gym process. You must protect yourself as much as you can.

This might sound a little funny and like it should be common sense, but it's worth saying here: make sure you are doing honest business.

There are four types of businesses entities you can register, including:

1.   S corporation

2.   C corporation

3.   Limited liability company (LLC)

4.   Sole proprietorship

I run an S corporation, which has many great tax benefits. I learned about the benefits of registering as an S corporation after talking to my accountant, who also serves as my bookkeeper. Before I learned about it, I paid a big price for my ignorance. So talk to the right people right from the beginning!

I didn't know the best way to file my business taxes, so I ended up paying much higher taxes than I needed to. If someone had sued the gym for something, I would have paid an even bigger price, as I would have been personally liable for a lawsuit.

In the early days, a new client came to me and claimed his back was hurting because of his training with me. Luckily I saw on his social media page that on that same day, he did a spin class for an hour and did all kinds of crazy jumps. I knew he couldn't have been hurt in my class because he only did one free session, and I gave him a light training. He wrote me a check, but then he changed his mind about the training. At this point, I realized how vulnerable my setup was, so I decided to protect myself as much as I could.

I am not an attorney, and this is not legal advice. I recommend you consult your lawyer and your accountant for the best advice here, but I'll talk you through some of the basic concepts.

Sole proprietorships are the simplest and cheapest option when you're looking to start a business. It costs little to start—but they don't protect you from personal liability.

An **LLC** is a lot like a corporation, but it's more flexible in terms of management and taxation. You can create an LLC by filing documents with the state and paying a fee for filing. This kind of filing gives you some legal protection.

It starts to get a little more complicated when you talk about **C corporations** and **S corporations**. The biggest difference between the two is how they are taxed, which is something you want to discuss with your accountant and your lawyer.

In addition to tax benefits, filing as an LLC, C corporation, or S corporation may help to keep you from being personally on the hook for business liabilities. Consult with your attorney or accountant to find the right entity structure for you.

With any of these business entities, you also need to pay a nominal fee for a local business license (this often starts under $100 for the first year). Check with your city or county.

FINANCES

If you don't keep track of how much money you're making, you have no idea if your business is successful. I don't just mean that you should know the total amount of your sales or the gross revenue. You also need to know what your net profit is. If you don't, there's no way you will be able to accurately tell what's working and what isn't. You need to know that so you can figure out how to do more of what's working to grow your business.

Here are some basic steps I recommend you take to get your financial house in order, and as soon as you can afford to, get a bookkeeper to help you on a monthly basis with this.

Keep important numbers front and center. I have a SixPax metrics spreadsheet where I keep all my important numbers, including total gross revenue, expenses, profit, marketing, payroll, new leads, new clients, and terminations. These things are important to me. Ask your bookkeeper to give you a monthly report and compare them with earlier months (and years) to find all the places you can improve. I also keep my net worth tracked on a free app called Mint.com. I check this obsessively every morning. I always know my numbers.

Pay your taxes. Follow the law. Pay your bills on time. Build a reputation of being very honest and straightforward. You will be tempted many times to do the wrong thing, but it is never worth it.

I had friends who tried to give me advice on how to cheat the system and pay less in taxes. That may have offered a short-term reward, but it would have had long-term impacts. If you report high income, sure you pay more in taxes, but remember that when you go to the bank to apply for a loan to expand your gym or to buy a house, they'll always look at your tax returns first, and if you're not reporting your proper income and not paying your taxes, you're going to be denied that loan.

Being honest has been a great strategy for me. When you are honest, you attract more money and good will.

SIXPAX TAX TIPS

While I think trying to cheat the system ultimately isn't worth it, that doesn't mean I think you should pay more than you need to. Here are a few ways gym owners can save money on their taxes.

1. As mentioned above, meet with your accountant or attorney and create a proper business entity. Not only will you limit your liability, but you may also enjoy lower tax rates.

2. Rearrange your affairs for maximum tax savings. Can you use that extra room in your house as a home office? I built a gym in my garage and called it a SixPax garage. I use it to shoot videos and plan to offer a training session at my home as a reward for SixPax's member of the month for their hard work. If you use a portion of your house for your work, talk to your accountant about writing off that space.

3. Document your expenses well. My accountant gives me a monthly report with exact numbers.

4. Be punctual. File all returns and pay all taxes due (income, payroll, sales, etc.) on time. This way, you avoid expensive late filing and payment penalties and interest. A bookkeeper helps tremendously with all of this.

5. Find a good accountant. You might be able to train them in exchange for their service.

EMERGENCY FUND

As soon as your business starts making a little extra money, start putting some of it away for emergency funds. Even something as small as a couple hundred dollars a month is a smart move. Having savings gives you security and peace of mind and allows you to make better decisions. Make it a goal to save six months worth of business and personal expenses in case something unexpected comes up.

Let me share a story with you about why this is helpful. Back in 2020, SixPax was doing great. When March came around, we were going stronger than ever. I bought a house the year before and did my best to save everything I had, but I spent all my money on remodeling. I started saving money for refinancing so I could show them I had the reserves to qualify. But on March 15, our county mandated all gyms shut down immediately to slow the spread of COVID-19. Suddenly, I had zero dollars coming in! Most gyms were shut down for many months. Huge chains like Gold's Gym, Flywheel, and 24 Hour Fitness filed for bankruptcy. GNC was next. I started seeing gyms change their business models by trying to switch to online training, reacting in panic.

I talked to my mentor to ask his advice on what I should do. He asked me if I had any savings. I told him I did. I could handle three months of a total shutdown.

He told me to focus on other parts of the business I'd been postponing, like writing this book, instead of wasting time on changing my business model for this short interruption. Because of my savings and that wise advice, I was able to focus on something that could add more value to SixPax and benefit me more in the long run. Three months later, I was only allowed to reopen outdoors, so I moved all my equipment outside, and even with the three-month long shutdown, and mega gyms going bankrupt, we went on to have our biggest growth year ever.

CREDIT SCORE

I'm always amazed when I see how many people ignore this important part of financial growth. It is so important for you to have a good credit score. If you don't, that's okay! There are many ways to improve it. Do your research, talk to companies that help people improve their credit scores, and then protect it with everything you have.

When it comes to leasing or buying a space, you will have a much better chance of getting that deal and getting a lower interest rate as well if you have a good credit score.

Here are seven ways to increase your credit score fast:

1. Correct all errors on your credit reports. Seventy-nine percent of all credit reports have errors that can lower the score.[12] Visit CreditHeroScore.com for a copy of your credit reports and scores from all three bureaus and look for the errors. Look specifically for personal information or negative items that are incorrect; accounts listed as "settled," "paid derogatory," or "paid charge-off"; or anything other than "current" or "paid as agreed" if you paid on time and in full. Accounts that are still listed as unpaid that were included in a bankruptcy should be marked as $0. Negative items older than seven years (10 in the case of bankruptcy) should not be listed. When you find an error, write the credit bureau that is reporting it to ask for its removal.

2. Be sure that proper credit lines are posted on the credit reports. So go through the entire report and make sure they are correct.

An incorrect credit limit can lower your score.

3. If you have negative marks on the reports, negotiate with the creditor or lender to remove them. If you are a longtime customer, and it's something simple like a one-time late payment, and the account is still open, a creditor will often wipe it away to keep you as a loyal customer.

4. Pay all credit cards and revolving credit down to below 30 percent of the available credit line and never spend more than that (even if you pay the bill off in full every month). This is the magic percentage to raise your score.

5. Never close old credit card accounts, as that will hurt your score. If you have old credit card accounts that you want to stop using, cut up the cards or hide them in a drawer, and keep the accounts open.

6. Avoid applying for new credit. Each time you apply for new credit, your credit score suffers. Also, never co-sign for anyone.

7. Maintain at least three revolving credit lines and one active (or paid) installment loan. The credit scoring system wants to see that you maintain a variety of credit accounts. If you do not have three active credit cards, you might want to open some (but keep in mind that if you do, the score will drop slightly for a few months).

SAFETY TIPS

Have automatic external defibrillators (AEDs) and know how to use them in emergencies.

AED devices are available in many facilities now for quick responses in the event of cardiac emergencies. You'll want to be certified in both AED and CPR if you can, including CPR for children and first aid.

Have a fire extinguisher on hand as well.

INSURANCE

Early on, I only had liability insurance to protect myself. I didn't have much money, so I didn't get any other insurance. Later I learned that property insurance was important when it came to protecting your equipment and your space in case of theft, fire, or other mishaps.

Make sure you cover everything when it comes to insurance. Don't try to cut corners. This is a dangerous game to play.

There's some kind of insurance package out there for everything, but here are a few kinds of coverage you may want to consider, depending on the needs of your gym:

- → General liability
- → Workers' compensation
- → Equipment coverage
- → Property coverage
- → Professional liability

Basically, every business—especially gyms—should have general liability insurance. If you own a home, you may want to consider asking your agent for an umbrella policy. These will help to protect your assets in the event that you or your business gets sued.

Worker's compensation and unemployment insurance are also required by most states if you have employees. Some states require this even if you're the only person on the payroll.

I recommend checking with your lawyer to see what policies you need, what policies might be beneficial for your specific gym, and which policies you can do without.

I got lucky with my lawyer. One of my clients and good friends referred me to a good lawyer who specializes in business who he said would ultimately save me a lot of money.

But if you don't have a referral, where should you start? I recommend you start by finding a general business lawyer. Many lawyers tend to specialize in specific fields, such as employment, taxes, or real estate, but you should start by finding someone to offer good general counsel.

You can also ask around to get referrals. There are many online directories out there, too.

You'll want to check any reviews that are publicly available and make sure the lawyers your considering don't have any ethical complaints against them.

From there, you can schedule a meeting to see if they are a good fit for you and your business. A good business lawyer should understand the fitness industry and have a good grasp of your specific situation.

CHAPTER 24

MY ROLE AS A TRAINER

I take my role as a trainer very seriously, and people can sense that. I train hard myself, and I am always dieting. SixPax Gym is my life 24/7.

My routine looks like this:

→   5:30 a.m. Wake up and eat breakfast

→   6 a.m. Train clients

→   8:30 a.m. Eat

→   9:30 a.m. Train clients

→   11:30 a.m. Train myself heavy and hard, do cardio

→   1:30-4 p.m. Eat, shower, nap

→   4-8 p.m. Train clients

→   8:30 p.m. Eat

→   9-11 p.m. Read a book or work on the business

I am a machine! I am on a set schedule, and everyone knows my timetable. People watch me practice exactly what I preach. I work hard to keep my clients accountable, but if I am going to have any credibility with them, I have to keep myself accountable first.

So many trainers out there try their best to get more clients and make more money, but they forget about themselves. They get so busy hustling all day and helping clients that they let themselves go. Before they know it, six months pass, and they're in a bad place!

If that sounds familiar, consider this your wake-up call. You have to take your own health seriously if you want your clients to take you seriously.

When I started to get ready for bodybuilding shows, it motivated my clients to see my regimen. I was in the gym right alongside them, doing all those things I asked them to do. I trained with intensity, cut out carbs, and did cardio for one to two hours a day. At that point, I was training six days a week. About 18 hours before the competition, I cut water and carb loaded.

But what if I lost? My mentor, bodybuilding legend Tom Platz, told me that even if I lost, it would be worth it to have my clients come. Platz was a renowned bodybuilder in the 1970s and 1980s. He was named Mr. Universe in 1980 and finished third place at the 1981 Olympia.

Me winning "Overall Champion" at Gold Coast Classic

"They are all living through you when you're on stage," he said to me. "Make it fun for them. They'll enjoy the show because of you."

My clients loved it! They cheered me on and showed up at my competition, though I was worried about having so many people come at first. It was an awesome experience.

Thinking back to my first show in America, no one came for me then. I was alone. I remember driving home alone with my trophy. No one was there to celebrate that win with me. No one even knew or cared that I did a show. I got home and had tilapia for dinner as usual. When I look back, I realize I expected loneliness. I thought that was part of the journey to greatness, and I told myself I could handle the pain. But now I had a team cheering me on! The whole gym was happy for me! All that hard work paid off.

By letting my clients into my own process, they could see I walked the walk. They came away with an even greater appreciation for my expertise. So, I was able to push them to places they never thought were possible.

TRAINING IS LIFE

Being a great leader means you need to show everyone that this is your life. That must be reflected in your lifestyle outside the gym, too. I'm not saying you need to walk around wearing muscle shirts and showing off your gains, but your life should reflect what you value.

As a trainer and a leader, I stay away from too many hobbies. I put all my energy into building my gym. I recommend you do the same.

To stay focused on your goal, I recommend you study successful people. Study those who have failed or might be about to fail. Always ask this question: Is what I'm doing benefiting my gym or not?

If you're partying and drinking, you aren't training very hard! If your friends are begging you to do those things with them, they are pulling you down! Get rid of them. That's real focus.

YOUR ATTITUDE

A wise person once told me trainers are a lot like superheroes—people come to feed off our energy. That's a great thing if you have good energy. People will keep coming for that if you are free of problems in your personal life—don't ever talk about your personal problems with clients, and don't complain about politics or other things.

Keep your own personal issues to yourself so your clients can use their time at the gym to focus on their own health. This will make your gym always look like heaven.

MAKE FRIENDS WITH OTHER SUCCESSFUL BUSINESS OWNERS

If you are an entrepreneur driven to succeed, your friends, family, and most people will never be able to relate to you. They may be unsupportive of your dream, or even worse, when you become successful, they may get jealous or angry. This is a sad fact about the road to success. Try to find other positive, success-driven entrepreneurs in your area that you can connect with and share stories with. Even though they may have completely different businesses, you will have more in common than you think, especially if they have customers. You need to have an outlet to share what you're going through with other people who understand and have been in your shoes.

I'm very lucky to have great friends who run successful businesses. When I talk to them about my struggles, they can all relate, encourage, and support me.

Every Sunday, I go for a ride on my Harley-Davidson with my friend and mentor, Daniel Rosen. We have breakfast and talk about our businesses. It's my favorite part of the week. We swap stories about our challenges, share useful contacts, refer or recommend various people or services, and more. Daniel owns a software company, which is very different from a gym, but many of his challenges as a business owner and entrepreneur are identical to mine.

BE HUMBLE

Remember, you're just starting out! By living a humble life, you will save a lot of money, and your clients won't think they're overpaying. They will feel like you are one of them.

I've seen trainers at other gyms driving expensive sports cars and wearing fancy clothes. It didn't make clients trust them more—instead, it did the opposite. New clients were intimidated by the look and didn't even want to approach them.

I've seen other trainers act like rappers or gangsters. They wear hoodies and walk around acting tough. While teenagers might think that's cool, the people who can afford your services will be turned off.

The bottom line is: you are a businessperson, and you must be approachable.

Client testimony: *Barak Sharpe*

In July 2016, I was reaching rock bottom in my personal life. I just found out I was getting a divorce after nearly 20 years of marriage, and I was almost 60 pounds overweight. After a week of grieving my failed marriage, it was time to make a change. I decided to find a personal trainer and commit to a month. I figured this would be enough time to establish a new healthy routine of exercise and eating clean. I reasoned that after a month of consistency, I would be able to continue on my own.

I did a quick search on Yelp and came across a five-star review of SixPax Gym. An image appeared of a smiling bodybuilder with a handlebar mustache promising in just 30 minutes, three times a week, he could give you a complete body transformation. I was skeptical, to say the least, but decided to take advantage of his free initial session.

The next day, I walked into the gym and was greeted by Siavash. He was very welcoming, and his gym had an instant feeling of community. This place felt special!

Siavash asked me what my goals were. I told him I was going through an unexpected divorce, and that I had let myself go physically.

I said, "I want to look like a guy on the cover of *Men's Health*."

He said, "No problem! Now grab that sledgehammer, and let's get to work." Thirty minutes later, I was soaking wet from sweat and exhausted from 30 minutes of training. Siavash approached the training with no-nonsense and no gimmicks—just old-fashioned hard work with compound exercises.

I told him right then and there that I was ready to become a member! I was no longer interested in only committing to one month with a trainer. I was going to become a long-term member, part of the SixPax family.

During the first month, I dropped 20 pounds! Siavash encouraged me every step of the way. At times, he used tough love, telling me there were "no excuses." At other times, he used encouragement and a realistic attitude, knowing that we all slip from time to time. "Don't dwell on the mistakes—fix it and move on."

By year's end, I was in the best shape of my life. In that short amount of time, Siavash took me from six foot one at 240 pounds to 185 pounds with 7 percent body fat!

Siavash taught me that training is an outward manifestation of the power and strength of our mind. Do we have what it takes to do simple things like eating clean, nutritious food as a fuel source to nourish our engines? Or is the momentary enjoyment from bad food worth the fantastic sense of self, accomplishment, power, and success that comes from training our bodies to look how we envision?

If we can harness that power with our minds, we can do the same in our relationships and work. We can accomplish anything we want in life. Siavash instilled in me a sense of pride and a renewed love of training, with catch-phrases like "Never settle," "Where the mind goes, the body follows," "Iron sharpens iron," and, of course, the iconic "Five more!"

Saying SixPax Gym changed my life is an understatement. Not only did I gain my health and reach my physical goals, but I also gained a family and a lifelong friendship with Siavash: a man I am proud to call my brother.

Something else happened. Siavash helped me find and become the best version of myself. In doing so, I met and fell in love with my soul mate. I know that without Siavash's mentorship, I could not have found my wife. Cheryl saw in me a version of me that was worthy of her—the best version of myself: a SixPax warrior.

Barak Sharpe (before and after)

PART FOUR
Grow

CHAPTER 25

CRAFT A MISSION STATEMENT

It can feel weird to come up with a mission statement. You might, like I did, feel like you're trying to create an ad for your gym. But it's not an ad. A mission statement is the heart and soul of your company, and it guides the direction of your business.

When crafting a mission statement, answer these questions:

→   Who do you help?

→   How do you help them?

→   What is the change you want to make?

→   How will you know you are successful?

SIXPAX GYM MISSION

Our mission statement is the most important document at our company. My team takes turns reading our mission statement at the start of every meeting. We all believe in it, we base all decisions on it, and it's posted on our wall in our office reminding us who we are, how we got here, and where we're going. Read it loud and proud.

We help busy professionals who have sacrificed their health to get ahead in business

We help them by creating the training and regimen to lose weight and gain muscle in record time.

The change we want to make is for our clients to fall in love with themselves, gain confidence, and become SixPax warriors.

We'll know we're successful when we are known worldwide as the most successful small gym in America.

STRONG COMPANY VALUES

All great organizations have strong company values. It's important to list those out and keep them top of mind. Why? They can:

- → Help your team make decisions
- → Align your team
- → Improve motivation
- → Communicate your principles to clients
- → Help you to attract the right employees

These are the SixPax Gym values:

1. **We over-deliver value**

   Our proven SixPax system is designed with one purpose: to deliver big results! For over ten years, we have helped thousands of clients lose weight and feel amazing. Our mission is to help our SixPax Warriors achieve their biggest goals.

2. **Diversity**

   We respect effort. No matter what race, gender, religion, language, who we date or love, we are all equal here.

3. **Authentic, friendly support**

   We firmly believe in and practice supporting our clients with authentic, friendly, and professional support. We admire and appreciate our clients for wanting to make physical fitness an integral part of their lives. Our team is here to serve, motivate, and focus on achieving the best version of yourself.

4. **Judgment-free zone**

   We have seen it all, and we do not judge—we only care about your goals and helping you achieve them. We believe that different values and the right to have differences of opinion make the world a richer place. Be who you are and allow others to be themselves.

5. **Living our truth**

   At SixPax Gym, we live what we preach. Every member of our SixPax team lives the same healthy, active lifestyle that we recommend to our SixPax warriors.

6.   **Changing lives**

We are client-focused, which means genuinely putting the client first. We proactively listen to clients' problems and find solutions. Each client is a potential success story. "Small Gym, BIG Results" means changing the lives of our clients, our team, our families, our communities, and the world...in every way we can.

Make sure you are practicing what you preach, and it all starts at the top with you, the CEO. You set the tone for the rest to follow.

CHAPTER 26

HAVE A SYSTEM

In order for your clients to have a good, consistent experience at your gym, you must have a system. That way everyone is on the same page, your clients know what to expect, and your team knows what they're supposed to do.

Imagine you go to a personal trainer, and one day he is all pumped up and ready to go. He gives you a bottle of water and a towel before you start, then you train hard. He's watching you on every rep and pushing you to do better. You finish training with a big smile on your face. He gives you a protein shake and praises a job well done. You have a great time!

The next time you go in, he's on his phone and he waives you in without a word. You start training a couple minutes late, and he rushes you to start and get pumped up. This time, he doesn't offer you a towel or a water bottle. You train hard, and you enjoy it well enough, so you come back again.

The third time you show up, he starts on time, but he's in a bad mood. He's not pumped up. He doesn't offer you water to start or a shake to finish. Every single time, the experience has been different. At some point, you ask yourself what's missing, and you probably don't come back.

You have to map out everything and simplify it as much as you can so the experience at your gym is consistent. People need to know what they can expect when they come to train with you.

I have created a system that is so easy to follow for clients and trainers alike. When we train upper body, we know exactly what to start with and what to finish with! If one trainer takes over another trainer's session 10 minutes into training, he knows exactly how to continue the class without any interruption. Every single section has been systemized leaving nothing to chance. Even water breaks are scheduled into the training for us. Both clients and trainers understand what they are in for and what's coming next.

When every trainer knows the basics, you can then assign them different responsibilities according to their strengths and weaknesses. If I know Trainer A isn't good with sales but he is great at correcting clients' form and teaching them techniques, I will have him focus on that. If Trainer B is great at sales, I will have him focus on that area.

The systemization will help your trainers feel empowered and capable of handling their job duties, and the more specialized responsibilities and duties will help them feel like they are accomplishing something and making a difference.

CHAPTER 27

BUILDING A DOCUMENTED PROCESS

It's important to build out documented processes. When starting a business, people often want to skip over this part because it feels complicated, but I promise you that processes set you free.

Since I have built repeatable processes, I have been able to step away from working on the floor and can instead focus on growing SixPax Gym. That's what makes the business successful and consistent—it's also what gives you, the business owner, ultimate freedom.

I have touched on this a little, but I want to dive deeper to take you to the next level.

Do you know why a hamburger at McDonald's or a cup of coffee at Starbucks tastes the same no matter where you are in the world? It's because they are masters of creating a process. This is the key to having a successful and scalable business.

When I first started out, I didn't have this. The uncertainty and irregularity created chaos, which stunted the growth of my business. I had to learn to create my processes the hard way, by trial and error and a lot of mistakes. I relied on my gut for everything. This made it difficult to teach others how to do what I did or how to think like me—that meant I had to be at the gym all the time to handle everything that came up. And a lot came up between signing up new clients, replying to emails, selling, and even training people. It was all me. That might feel good in the beginning, but you will quickly realize how much pressure that puts on you and how fast that can burn you out. Your clients will also eventually notice that you don't have the structure in place to create a consistent experience for them.

Once I created a documented process and a policy for everything in the gym, anyone on my team could replicate what I did. They knew how to close a customer, respond to problems, and make decisions for me. Suddenly I was able to take days off and even go on vacation without worrying about the business. Processes set me free. I want to make sure they do the same for you.

Write your processes down and use flow charts so that others can follow them. Write your policies down so that others can make decisions for you. Once these are in place and working, don't be tempted to change them.

I struggled with this in the early days. If there was a sudden dip in clients, a slow month during the holiday season, fewer leads because of a bad ad agency, or one client with an issue, I used to make drastic changes to my business out of my own anxiety, and everything would fall apart, including the good parts that had always been working! After making this mistake over and over, I finally learned to trust my processes implicitly.

This has saved me a lot of time and energy over the years, and it will for you too. Trust and follow your processes. That's the only way to build a successful business and consistent client experience.

What do these processes look like? I'll share my key processes with you. Feel free to use them.

WHEN A LEAD FIRST COMES IN

When leads come in, we have a nurturing system in place. We call them as quickly as we can (within five minutes, if possible) to book them for a free session. If we don't reach them immediately, we text them and then follow up through our email automation, a 30-day nurture sequence, which has been set up in GoHighLevel software.

When trainers follow up with leads through phone calls, they have a script to follow so they know what to say and what to ask in order to guide a client into scheduling their free session.

Here is an example of the first email that is sent right after someone signs up for a free session:

> **Subject:** Transformation Session Confirmed. Congratulations!
>
> **Pre text:** Here's what you can expect & how to prepare...
>
> **Copy:**
>
> Hi! I'm Siavash, certified trainer and founder of SixPax Gym.
>
> I want to take a second to congratulate you on scheduling your **FREE Transformation Session!**

During this session you'll get:

- ☑ Training with a professional certified trainer to see where your strengths and weaknesses are.

- ☑ A full body fat scan to analyze where you're at right now and how to improve.

- ☑ A one of a kind SixPax Gym training shirt!

And the best part is...

By the end of your session, you'll have a foolproof, PROVEN plan!

No more guessing. No more trial and error. No more questioning or wasting time.

You'll know EXACTLY how our members have...

- → *Lost over 8,528+ pounds*

- → *Cured health issues like high blood pressure*

- → *Taken back their health, fitness, energy, and future...*

And how you can too!!

So, here's how you can get the most from your Transformation Session...

From now until you step into SixPax Gym, jot down in your phone or in a notebook everything you eat.

If it's a Big Mac, write it down.

A salad? Write it down.

Brownie, apple, protein shake, beer...

Write. It. Down.

Why?

Because when you bring your notes with you to your session, I'll look through them with you and make a practical food plan for your lifestyle.

Now, if that feels vulnerable, don't worry! I'm not here to judge, and trust me, I've seen it ALL!

Good, bad, or otherwise, bring it in and let's set the foundation for *your future fit self*!

Deal?

I hope so!

I'm excited! I'll see you soon!

Small Gym, BIG Results.
Siavash Fashi
CEO/Founder of SixPax Gym

PS: Wondering what's possible?

Check out one of our SixPax warriors, Eric! He lost 104 pounds in just eight months!

"JOINING SIXPAX HAS BEEN A LIFE-CHANGING EXPERIENCE! When I joined SixPax Gym eight months ago I was in terrible shape—293 pounds, high blood pressure, slow and sluggish, and at 46 years old. With the help, guidance and incredible knowledge and training skills of Siavash and the SixPax family, I am now a changed man! As of today, I have lost 104 pounds! I no longer have high blood pressure and I am in the best shape of my life. Thank you, Siavash and Peri at SixPax Gym for making me a SixPax warrior!!!"

DELIVERY OF SERVICE

Once we book a potential client for a free session, we make sure our delivery is consistent. We ask them to arrive 15 minutes early for the session. As soon as the client walks in, we greet them. We then weigh them, measure their body fat, ask a few questions about their current situation, and have them sign the waiver (on an iPad with the SignNow app). From there, they go into training, where even their routines have been documented. Once a trainer sees a new client is on the schedule, the trainer knows exactly what to do.

AFTER THE SESSION/CLOSING THE SALE

Once the free session is done, we sit down with the person and convert them into a client. Our sales script is documented so everyone can follow it and get the same results. This means I don't have to be at the gym having each one of these conversations myself! My trainers can do what I do and close sales at the same rate because I have documented everything for them. All they have to do is follow the process and enter the client's credit card into the system.

AFTER THE SALE

Once the sale is finalized, we give the client a free SixPax Gym T-shirt and send them an email with their food plan and schedule. We have a checklist for this to make sure we don't leave anything out. Nothing is worse than promising a client something simple like a food plan and then forgetting about it because you relied on your memory. A little mistake like this will affect your retention. It sends the message that you are not organized and you have a sloppy system. Here is my checklist. At SixPax, we make sure the list gets reviewed by two other trainers!

SixPax Gym Fitness Assessment

First Name: _____

Last Name: _____

Date: _____   Weight: _____

Height: _____   Body Fat %: _____

BMI: _____   Injuries: _____

Schedule (what works for client): _____

How did client hear about SixPax? _____

Administration Checklist

☐ Joined   ☐ Reason for not joining:

Add client info into notes _____

Set up schedule and send to client _____

Send client diet plan _____

Payment setup _____

Great businesses don't happen by accident. They are built through documented repeatable processes.

Even your hiring process must be documented. Here's an example of what an ad for hiring might look like:

SIXPAX GYM

JOB DESCRIPTION:

We are looking for a Head Coach/Trainer to encourage and support our clients to change their lives!

OVERVIEW:

SixPax Gym is the most successful small gym in America.

We help busy professionals who have sacrificed their health to get ahead in business.

We help them by creating the training and regimens to lose weight and gain muscle in record time.

The change we want to make is for our clients to fall in love with themselves, gain confidence, and become SixPax warriors.

We'll know we're successful when we are known worldwide as the most successful small gym in America.

ROLES AND RESPONSIBILITIES:

Promptly start, lead, and end 30-minute, semi-private class sessions of predesigned SixPax system interval training.

Check in with current clients to keep them accountable.

Attend regular team meetings and training.

WE WANT OUTGOING AND PASSIONATE INDIVIDUALS WHO:

Have a great personality!

Take pride in helping people reach their ultimate fitness goals.

Want to make an impact in the world and change lives.

QUALIFICATIONS AND REQUIREMENTS:

Friendly and open demeanor. (We really mean this—authenticity is one of our CORE values, we have a small team.)

Certification after one month of SixPax training experience.

Excellent verbal communication skills.

SixPax Gym is an equal opportunity employer and is committed to working with a diverse staff. We hire for talent and drive, and we value members by work deliverables and passion. No matter what race, color, creed, religion, gender, or sexual orientation, we are all equal here.

We encourage every talented and qualified person to apply.

PROCESS FOR ANSWERING THE PHONE

Always smile and have good energy when answering the phone. Even if callers can't see your face, they can get a sense of how you feel. Be loud and clear. Don't talk fast.

Start with stating your name, the location they called, and ask how to help. For example, I would say this:

"Hi, this is Siavash at SixPax Gym. How can I help you?"

Listen to the question the caller is asking and thank them for reaching out.

If you don't know the answer to the question they are asking, or need more information, be curious. Ask them a few more questions to help you understand what they need. Keep it simple and talk about one subject at a time.

If they're calling for general information, tell them very simply what you do. I would answer this question like this:

"At SixPax, you come with a goal in mind and we will help you reach it with a practical food plan and training plan. We will help you to correct your form so you don't get injured. Plus, you'll have access to the gym seven days a week for cardio. We will sit down with you and come up with a plan. Try a free session to get a feel for us and how we train.

REFUNDS

As I mentioned earlier, you will have to deal with refunds. It's just part of the job. Give your trainers a clear script to follow when it comes up.

Refund the money right away. It doesn't matter if the client used all their sessions, has abused your system, or has been taking advantage of your kindness. I know it's painful. You worked hard for that money, but every once in a while you will come across an unreasonable client, and it's better to get rid of them quickly. Arguing with them will cost you more in the long run. Refund the money and focus on your great clients.

Be as polite as possible. Ask for feedback. Here's an example of what to say:

"I am sorry to see you go. I will stop the account and make sure you don't get charged going forward. I will refund you right away. Please give your bank five business days to process the refund. Thank you again for training with us. I am always here if you need me."

This sends the message that you care about changing people's lives more than anything else—and that's ultimately why we own a gym!

CHAPTER 28

GIVING BACK TO YOUR COMMUNITY

One of the best things that happened to me when I opened SixPax Gym was when the Pauly family joined. They have a 21-year-old son named Matt who has autism. He is very smart and always knew how to get away with stuff and would outsmart us all the time!

In the beginning, I was nervous about how I should go about training him, but after a few sessions, we got to know each other. I made it fun. We did a lot of different things, and I always tried to make the training something Matt would enjoy. He lost 30 pounds, and his parents lost weight as well. Matt's mom, Tami, was so excited about their progress she introduced me to a special needs program. I signed up a kid named Stephen. I loved seeing him at the gym! He lost a total of 103 pounds, and we ended up in the newspaper for his success.

My team and clients all love Matt and Stephen.

They put flyers up in the school that said we train special needs kids and would give them discounts.

Then Andrew joined us!

Andrew's mom is very active, always taking him to basketball games or other fun things. Andrew is a superstar. This kid is so strong—he is built like a brick house! He is all about having fun, and then he will go to sleep right after training.

They inspire all of my clients. Having them around changes the atmosphere at the gym for the better.

Remember, your gym can do real good and have a real impact in your community. It can be worth taking on something that might be out of your comfort zone!

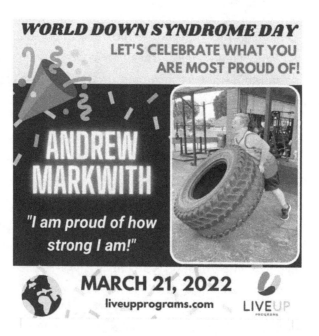

CHAPTER 29

HOW TO BECOME A CELEBRITY OF YOUR TOWN

When I opened a gym, my goal was to let people know I existed and was ready to get them into shape. I was in L.A., the land of movie makers and Hollywood legends, so I knew it would take something special to stand out.

I started off trying to get the word out about my gym with the help of local bodybuilders. I asked them to come to my gym and let me be in their videos so I could get exposure for my gym. Back then I thought my success depended on them. If I got lucky, they'd talk about my gym for a few seconds. Some wanted me to pay them to come to my gym and include it in their videos.

My aha moment came when I realized I was the one in charge of my own destiny. I realized I knew more about my business than anyone else, so it made sense for me to make my own videos.

My videos are always less than 60 seconds long. They are short and to the point. I make them early in the morning, at 6 a.m. when the gym opens up. Every day I talk about a different subject. I started by educating people about our system, who we are, why I opened SixPax, and more. I highlighted my SixPax Warrior wins, my own lifestyle, my diet, my dog, places I visited, and more. I made celebrities out of clients who were successful.

I posted those videos on Instagram and Facebook. The response was amazing! Clients loved them.

It's okay if you find yourself repeating stories, because so many new people watch those videos that you never know who is hearing it for the first time. Don't worry about people's opinions or criticisms. If your intention is to help people, that's what matters.

In the beginning, I was so self-conscious about my English, my grammar, and the way I looked at the camera. I eventually learned that none of that mattered. Now I view my accent as an asset. The things that make you unique help you to bring your own flavor to the game. This makes everything more real, intense, and engaging.

These videos, as with everything we do, should be simple, fun, and valuable.

One of the most important parts of making videos and posting pictures is consistency. You must have consistency with everything you do.

I often see people start making great content and then they disappear—and so do their leads!

Rain or shine, I am out there making videos about what we do.

One of the biggest benefits to posting videos of your clients training is retention. People love to watch themselves. They also love to watch people they know or can relate to.

You may make a mistake or say the wrong thing, but it's okay! Keep practicing and your videos will get better. You will grow alongside the business.

Announcing weight loss stats on Facebook Live.

One popular, regular video feature I did spotlights the weight loss board I made. I hung the board in the gym, and I regularly update the total weight lost at SixPax. I then make a video announcing the clients who lost weight, and the clients love it. I got the idea when I watched a car auction in Texas.

You are changing people's lives. Be loud and proud about it!

Trainer testimonial: *Bill Tenwick*

I describe SixPax Gym as a very attractive force. It's not just a gym with weights and treadmills. It's a higher power, it's a culture, it's a place where good things happen to good people. It's a place where you go to get motivated and workout hard by taxing your muscles to the extreme. The rewards come and reveal themselves in many different ways. Not only do people, who are committed to the SixPax method, improve their physique, but they also build on their inner confidence and self-esteem. The committed member glows with vitality and good health. As a trainer, I see this, and there is no better feeling than to help people change their lives and help them reach their full potential.

Coach Bill Tenwick

CHAPTER 30

CREATING AN ATMOSPHERE

I wanted to have an old-school gym—one that was a bit rough looking to send the message that we were all about hard work, not flash. I wanted it to be a place you could throw weights around without worrying about offending someone. I had the mats, I had the weights, I had the clients—how did I get that vibe?

I listened to a guy who talked about how Starbucks worked to craft its environment. He explained it was almost more of an atmosphere than a business.

I looked into it a little bit more. For years, Starbucks built the idea of a "third place" into its brand, referring to a place separate from work and from home where people can gather together and enjoy a sense of community.[13] The idea was that customers would be willing to pay a little more for their cup of coffee in exchange for the atmosphere and potential connections they might make and enjoy in that space.

That made so much sense! When I trained at Temple Gym in England, the roof was leaking, the benches were all torn up and put back together with duct tape, the dumbbells were loose from being thrown around, and the sound of iron rattling constantly rang through the space. It was a dungeon! The experience was insane! But once you went there, you got hooked. Nothing felt the same. I didn't want to train anywhere else, even though it was rough and ugly. It was real.

Now I needed to create the atmosphere.

STEP ONE: ADD SOMETHING UNIQUE

I hired a graffiti guy to tag the wall with a few positive slogans. People loved it. The gym was more colorful and helped people not to get bored looking around.

If the walls are boring, it's easy for people to just look at their phones or try to escape the space. Every minute seems to last an hour.

But imagine your friend had to go to a motorcycle shop to get some repairs done, so you tag along. While he is dealing with the mechanic, you walk around. You see many cool parts of different bikes being used to create art pieces, pictures of girls on magazines on the walls, old motorcycles on display up front. It looks cool! So, you start taking pictures of this cool spot and sharing it on social media. Bingo! Now people are marketing your business for you because your place is unique.

STEP TWO: ENHANCE THE ENVIRONMENT

The space was small, so I knew I had to make it look larger. I put two mirrors on a wall against each other. They gave the place depth and made the gym look bigger. Plus, you can't have a bodybuilding gym without mirrors! You have to check out those muscles every couple of minutes.

I sat down and designed the gym in many different ways so I could squeeze in more equipment without making the gym feel too crowded.

In the end, everything was a couple of steps away, so the clients didn't waste any time. They loved it!

I put all the leg equipment in one area, so they were just a few feet away from each other. That way, clients could do a superset, or I could have clients all doing legs at the same time and I could keep an eye on them. I recommend always leaving the middle empty so there is room for people to space themselves out as much as they like and move around while other clients are lifting.

STEP THREE: BE MOTIVATIONAL

When I was a kid, my walls at home were covered in bodybuilding pictures. I know many of you did the same thing! You put a bunch of pictures on your wall to create an atmosphere you liked, signaling it was your room. Maybe it reminded you that you wanted that Ford GT40 or that amazing six-pack. Maybe you also put up pictures of your friends and family to remind you about what was important in life.

The gym is the same. You want that space to feel like home to you and your clients. Decorate it with motivational posters. Put up photos of clients or significant achievements. This will help make people feel like the space is for them.

This is the most important one: Create a wall for before and after pictures of your clients. I call ours the warrior's wall. As soon as you enter the gym you should see it. It motivates clients to work hard to end up on the wall, and visitors are inspired by it and want to be part of our community. Not only does this look awesome, but it's an extension of your website and a part of your sales funnel, because if it's displayed where all new potential clients must see it when they show up for a free session, it will help to close the deal by showing them 100 percent proof that your gym delivers results.

The Wall of Warriors

I also give out an award for member of the month. You can give out rewards such as private one-on-one sessions, cool hoodies with embroidery saying "member of the month," or something along those lines. The goal is for other clients and potential clients to see this as a sign of hard work and accomplishment.

CHAPTER 31

CLEANING YOUR GYM

This is a no-brainer, but trust me, too many gym owners make mistakes with this. They clean the gym once or twice a week, and they trust clients to keep the place clean. But this won't cut it.

You must clean your gym every single day, twice a day. Constantly wipe down machines and equipment between sessions. If you and your team are doing this all the time, it will train your clients to clean up after themselves too. You can put signs up telling people to wipe down machines, but unless you are setting an example, they probably won't do it.

If you're walking into the gym and you see trash in the parking lot, pick it up. If you're going to the bathroom and you see that it's dirty, clean it right away. In fact, check the bathroom every 30 minutes.

I recommend having a sheet to help keep your team accountable for these duties. Anyone doing the checks is responsible for signing the sheet.

Keep your office tidy. It's important not to have paperwork all over the place. That, too, sets an example.

Inside my office at SixPax Gym

CHAPTER 32

TV, MUSIC, AND AMENITIES

Some of this will come down to personal preference and what kind of atmosphere you want to create at your gym, but this is what I suggest to create an environment where clients are serious about working out.

When you go to big commercial gyms, you'll probably notice right away that they have flat screen TVs playing sports, news, or even cooking channels. It never made sense to me that people doing cardio would have to stare at delicious foods they couldn't eat. Some people feel like it's better to at least be burning calories rather than sitting on the couch watching TV at home, but I say no TVs!

At my gym, people are there to get results. I need them to focus. TV might make some aspects of the exercise a little more fun, but I think there are other ways you keep things lively. Besides, as soon as you get a TV, people will ask you to change the channel to something else. Hell no! You don't want to spend your time doing that. You need to stay focused on your clients, not the TV.

As far as music goes, I don't mind it. But I recommend keeping the volume at a reasonable level. I've been to some gyms that play such loud music I feel like I'm at a club. You want your clients to be able to hear you clearly. Plus, many of your clients won't like the music you play, no matter what it is. If it's too loud or has too much foul language, your clients will be annoyed.

Ultimately, you want your clients to spend more time focusing on their bodies, how they feel, and how much they enjoy your training than what channel to watch or what song to play.

On that note, many gyms will also include various amenities and will sell snacks, water, and more.

At SixPax, we keep it simple. We don't even sell water. Many people have suggested to me that I start selling products, but I don't. I'm a trainer. That's why I'm at the gym, so that's what I focus on. I like to have T-shirts on hand, and I give people a free one so they'll become a walking billboard advertising SixPax Gym, and I have a water fountain people are free to use.

Selling things like water can be a source of income if you're running a commercial gym with thousands of members, but if your gym has 100 to 150 people, you won't make enough money for it to be worth it, and suddenly you're focusing on product inventory, which is a waste of your time. If you want to grow your business, stay focused on the two most important things: offering amazing training and signing up more clients.

PART FIVE
Scale

CHAPTER 33

MARKETING YOUR GYM

I pass by gyms every day without even noticing them. If someone who has been obsessed with bodybuilding for most of his life can't tell that building is a gym, why would anyone else be able to? Marketing your location is critical for success.

My first location was a 1,000 square foot hole-in-the-wall. The front of the building was about the size of two garage doors. The door to the gym was broken, and the windows were cracked when I first took it over. We didn't stand out at all.

But that changed.

I fixed up the windows and bought a couple of cardio machines to put in front of them. I encouraged clients to come in and do cardio by the windows. The clients liked that they could see the sunlight, and people passing by saw others working out. It was a win-win situation! The big tires outside sent a message, too.

The first step to marketing your location is to make it look like the kind of place people want to be. But what comes after that? This is where many gym owners fall short.

LEAD GENERATION

To generate leads, you have to put yourself out there and make people curious about your service. This might include passing out business cards, creating Facebook ads, using Craigslist, Yelp, or more.

Here's the golden rule: Everyone within three feet of you should know what you do. I wear a SixPax T-shirt all the time. I have a big sign on my truck saying SixPax. The license plate on my car says SixPax. The license plate on my Harley says SixPax. I am in shape, which shows the kind of results you can get. Let everyone know what you do and be proud of it! Let them know you can serve them and help them get into great shape.

SixPax is everywhere!

You want to have as many leads as you can, because your chances of closing are higher when you do. It's a lot like asking someone out! You just need to ask more. Eventually someone will say yes! Or if you're more into fishing metaphors, think of it this way: use as many fishing poles as you can!

In the beginning, you'll have to put a lot of muscle in to create those leads. After you've made some money, you can delegate it to an agency to do it for you.

Remember, when I started out, I had no money, so I definitely wasn't spending a cent on Facebook ads! Instead, I walked around the neighborhood and introduced myself and my new gym. I talked to people as I went grocery shopping or stopped by restaurants. I let everyone within three feet of me know who I was and what I was doing!

It's also important to post on social media and invite people to come try out a free session. Have no money for ads? Post on social media three times a day. Tell your own story, tell client success stories, give fitness and nutrition tips, be the expert, share interesting things happening in your life and at your work, and always invite them to come have a free session at your gym. This not only works for me, but it also works for every gym owner that I've mentored. You want people to get a taste of your gym and build relationships with them. Even if they don't sign up to train, that relationship is an important networking connection.

Once you do start making money, I recommend that you set a monthly budget for marketing and lead generation.

Here are other ways I have generated leads:

→ Create a referral program incentive for your current clients to refer you more clients. I give $50 off to the client who referred and $50 off to the client who signed up.

→ Post pictures and videos on Facebook, Instagram, Yelp, YouTube, and TikTok daily. Advertise a free session.

→ Put your business cards and brochures up in grocery stores, coffee houses, and other local businesses with community bulletin boards. Use VistaPrint to produce them. This won't cost you much! On the back of my cards it says "Good For One Free Session."

→ Have a website. I use ClickFunnels—I love it!

→ Collect email addresses for your email list to market to. My email list is stored in Mindbody and GoHighLevel.

→ Call old clients who have stopped showing up and try to get them back in with a special offer once a year. I will offer my $299 per month package for only $99 for one month. Don't discount your prices too often. Have you ever seen a Ferrari on sale? Discounts every once in a while are fine to help jump-start clients who are hesitant, but don't rely on this.

→ Give out gift cards to your clients to give to their friends for a free consultation and free training session.

→ Give out gift cards to your network of business associates to hand out to their clients as a gift.

→ Go to chamber of commerce events and network. Meet new people every day. Join a business networking group. Refer leads to them first, then they will refer leads to you.

→ Prospect daily. Follow a script, and call your contacts to dig up leads of people they know that may benefit from your service. You may need to make 10 to 30 calls or emails a day for new leads.

→ Put a sandwich sign outside on both sides of the building so the traffic passing by or anyone stopped at a red light can see you're offering free 30-minute sessions.

You can do all of this on a budget. Remember, no one hands you a successful business. It's your job to make it successful. Consistent daily effort will increase your results.

PRESENTATION

Make a nice sign that is visible to people passing by. Put your logo and banners all around so people can't miss you.

It may take a couple months of branding before you see any returns, but don't give up!

CONSISTENCY IN MESSAGE

Have a clear, concise, consistent message. Can you describe your gym in one sentence?

I can. Small Gym, BIG Results!®

Once you have that message down, be in people's faces 24/7. Be loud, be proud—you are changing people's lives.

WEBSITE

Have a website. It doesn't have to be fancy—in fact, it should be simple enough that you can understand how it works and be able to make changes without needing a lot of help or expensive programmers. A simple website with a clear message and helpful information will close half the sales for you. Your site must answer all the basic questions about your gym, including where it's located, what your hours are, what your prices are, and what your methods are.

The most important part of your website is what visitors can see in the top section without scrolling. That area is called "above the fold"—a term left over from the newspaper industry, which had its important stories above the top half of the front page, where the paper folded, so it would be the first thing that catches people's eye.

So, the top section of your website should have the most important information about you and your gym. This should include a "call to action"—a button to sign up for a free session. That call-to-action button must be a very bright color to stand out from everything else in the page. That button should be on the page multiple times. Have it on top for the impulse buyers. Include it again further down the page to appeal to your logical buyers who scroll to learn more.

Make sure to include proof of your success, such as before and after pictures and testimonials. Make sure to always show real people, never stock photos or clip art fake people. Remember, it's not a pretty website that brings you business—it's your story, your authenticity, your social proof, and your call to action.

Your website must include your logo and brand colors, which you should be using with your ads, landing pages, and the gym itself for consistent branding.

I strongly suggest studying Russell Brunson's books to learn more about marketing. Here are some of his helpful titles:

→ *Dotcom Secrets: The Underground Playbook for Growing your Company Online with Sales Funnels.* Get it free at DotCom-Secrets.com

→ *Expert Secrets: The Underground Playbook for Converting Your*

Online Visitors into Lifelong Customers. Get it free at Expert-Secrets.com

→ *Traffic Secrets: The Underground Playbook for Filling Your Websites and Funnels with Your Dream Customers*. Get it free at TrafficSecrets.com

Once you start making money, you can hire someone to build you a better website and create various sales funnels for you. But before you do, always remember, a pretty website may not make you as much money as an ugly website, so be careful to not fix or change things that already work. Instead, focus on your next steps and moving forward on what you don't have yet, instead of going backward.

REVIEWS, REVIEWS, REVIEWS

Get as many reviews as you can. It's okay to ask people to leave them!

I typically ask people to leave reviews on SixPax Gym's Yelp page, Google page, or Facebook page.

Whenever I want or need to get motivated and excited about the gym, I look at our reviews on the following pages:

→ Yelp

→ Facebook

→ Google Reviews

→ My company website

These pages are full of people praising SixPax for changing their lives. Beyond the confidence boost, reviews are valuable to your business.

Why are reviews valuable? They help other people find the gym. Many clients tell me they decided to join SixPax after they saw so many five-star reviews.

I have seen some gyms try to imitate other businesses by getting reviews from clients right after they join or after just a couple sessions. To me, these reviews are meaningless.

People are excited in the beginning, and if you ask them to they will write a review in an attempt to build a relationship with you. Often, they are hoping this will get them better service. This is a good method if you are selling a product rather than a service like personal training.

You want your reviews to be as genuine as possible. You want the positive reviews to actually mean something. Mine do—and if I'm ever feeling down, I read my reviews and every single time they bring a tear to my eye because I know they are written with a full heart.

I recommend allowing your clients to train for a full month before either sending them an automated email or asking them in person to leave a review. Tell them they are your ideal clientele and that their review will help allow you to attract the right people and build a better community at the gym.

Once you get reviews, post them everywhere. Show the world how much you can help people. As part of this strategy, make sure to take before and after pictures of your clients so you can post those, too.

In the beginning, focus on getting positive reviews. After you start making money, you can start paying organizations like Yelp and Google to list your gym at the top of their page. Make sure to track the data and adjust your spending according to the results.

It's important to respond to all the reviews you get. Always reply to positive reviews and thank your clients for saying something positive and encouraging.

You will have clients who write bad reviews, but don't worry about it. Simply reply and say, "Thank you for bringing this to my attention. Your feedback allows me to make the gym better."

HANDLING NEGATIVE REVIEWS

Negative reviews are part of business. It's impossible to make everyone happy all the time, even if you try really hard to do so! So, what happens when you get a negative review?

First, stay calm. Slow down and never rush to react, even if your blood is boiling. You can use this situation for good, even if it feels bad in the moment. Take some time to put yourself in their shoes and understand their experience. This is the true test of an entrepreneur.

Answer the review quickly, thoughtfully, and honestly.

Publicly acknowledge that you aren't perfect. Be genuine when you apologize and address the complaint. Make a plan to do better. Offer some kind of credit or refund.

Remember, other people will now be reading this, so your response might not only turn a negative experience into a positive one, but it may also bring you other potential clients.

BEFORE AND AFTER PICTURES

This is the bread and butter of every small gym. It's the perfect way to show off results!

I have hundreds of before and after pictures. That's how I built a name for myself. People all across the community know that if they want results, they should go to SixPax. They know that they'll have to work hard, but they know it will pay off. Post these pictures everywhere—on your warrior wall, Yelp, Google, Facebook, and Instagram. Post them loud and proud!

Before and after pictures are the best social proof of what you have to offer your clients. At the first session, ask your clients if you can take a photo of them with their shirt off. Some people will feel uncomfortable with taking their clothes off because they've had self-image issues for many years. If they are embarrassed, simply ask them to take a picture at home on their first day in front of a white wall. Tell them to keep that picture so they can compare their progress to it every couple of months. It doesn't have to be fancy. Plan to take progress photos every month. When people lose weight, make them celebrities in your gym! Post their before and after pictures everywhere. They are your movement. Their stories will make your gym a part of a community of positive change.

TESTIMONIALS

Testimonials are proof that your services work. These are the kinds of things—more than any sales pitch—a future client will listen to.

Obviously, you have to earn your testimonials. Start by helping your clients change their lives and deliver results. After that, ask them to tell their story.

Once you get that testimonial, share it! Brag about your clients and the work they've done. Show the world, using Facebook, Instagram, Twitter, LinkedIn, and other platforms you use, that you're proud of what your client has been able to accomplish in your gym.

Make sure to include a link back to your website so future clients interested in taking steps to change their lives will know where and how to find you.

MERCHANDISE

Print out a simple T-shirt with your logo on it and give them out to your clients and to anyone else who shows an interest in your gym. Let them advertise for you! They will be proud to wear it because it shows they are part of a great community. But don't overspend on this—you aren't in the clothing business, after all.

Keep it consistent—just your logo and name of your town will do it.

MAKE VIDEOS

At first, I was hesitant to make videos. I was worried about my English, my grammar, and my accent. I worried people would make fun of me. Then, when I finally got the nerve to try it out, I bought a bunch of expensive camera gear, a fancy tripod, and the works. I wanted to have all the proper equipment before I started, so I shelled out thousands of dollars on it. But then I realized I didn't know how to use any of the gear, and it was too bulky to use while training people.

I eventually started using my iPhone, and it changed the way I do business forever. I started shooting short videos and posting them on Instagram and Facebook. Soon, I started getting good at it!

One of my clients, a producer of the MTV show *Teen Mom*, told me I should develop a tagline to use for the videos, so I did. I started saying, "Welcome to SixPax Gym" at the beginning of all my videos and ending them with, "I will see you at SixPax Gym, baby!" The tagline was simple, but it worked. People remember it. Now when I go shopping, people recognize me from the videos and shout, "SixPax Gym, baby!" Even my own clients started saying it.

Now I'm obsessed with making videos! The key is not to worry about being perfect. You will mess up on camera, and that's okay. When you start, your goal should be to practice and get more comfortable in front of the camera.

Getting likes and followers is nice, but your goal should be to bring information, value, and a little entertainment for your viewers. It helps the outside world see how busy your gym is and what kind of fun stuff your clients do.

Because I've had so much practice making videos, it's easy for me when the local news channels want to do an interview. As soon as the camera rolls, I am Mr. Hollywood! I'm ready to go because I've already practiced hundreds of times.

Once you start making these videos, you will start to find your own voice and your own style of talking. The goal is to be yourself and let people know you are here for them. Remember, having some rough edges makes you more relatable! Be as real as possible. Don't try to act rich or become a psychologist.

If I'm working with a client who has lost a lot of weight or has reached a goal important to them, I like to make a short video praising them and celebrating them.

I make videos of stuff outside the gym too to remind clients that I'm a real person. I show random stuff from my life, like food I'm eating, other people I do business with, videos from seminars I attend, and even some videos of my Harley rides. My most-liked videos are always of my dogs playing and having fun. The goal is to show my clients I'm just like them—I'm having fun and enjoying life while being healthy and fit.

Here are some video ideas to get you started:

→ Tell your story

→ Tell stories of client success

→ Tell your team members' stories

→ Show how much weight has been lost at the gym

→ Dance with dumbbells on TikTok

→ Give fitness and nutrition tips

BUSINESS CARDS

Have business cards, but keep them simple. Make sure all the information is easy to read. Make sure your logo stands out. Give your card out to everyone.

You can offer a free session on the back of your card, so they are more likely to keep it. Do not waste too much money on this. Keep it simple!

The back of my business card

WORK WITH OTHER BUSINESSES

I work with great massage therapists, chiropractors, acupuncturists, gym equipment suppliers, food service providers, and restaurants. I send my clients to them so they don't waste money on services that are subpar. When you work with the best, it adds value to your business as well.

Great business owners know the power of referrals. A good way to start is to ask if you can leave your flyers at their office and ask the other businesses to send people to you.

I recommend you try the services out yourself to see if they are worth it before sending your clients to another business. If they aren't good at what they do, don't work with them. You are here to build long-term relationships with your clients, and that system won't work if you refer them to bad places.

If you hear negative feedback from clients, stop referring people there until the problem is resolved.

PAID ADVERTISING

In my first four years of business, I didn't spend any money on paid advertising. The only things I spent money on were flyers and business cards, so don't worry if you don't have money in the beginning to think about this. But as soon as you do, this is one of the most important parts of your business.

I don't mean paying for random ads. These will be costly and won't be effective. I have done so much random advertising, and I wasn't able to track it. If you can't track it, it's like flushing your money away.

I recommend trying smaller, less expensive options. Facebook, Instagram and Google ads are a great way to go. You can get a lot of views, and you can target people close to your gym. You'll want to target your demographic or niche. For a simple ad, you might start by introducing yourself and your gym, and invite them to try a free session.

On Facebook, Instagram, and Google, you can also show ads to just the people who have already visited your site, so you haunt them wherever they go. This is called remarketing. This is done by adding a tracking pixel (from Facebook and Google) to your site and landing pages. Not only are remarketing ads much less expensive (because you are only advertising to people who have already visited your site or your offer), but they are quite effective. Make sure to create simple landing pages on your website for each platform so you can tell exactly which platform your leads are coming from *and* make sure you are following each platform's rules. A landing page is very simple, and it only does one thing. It collects the name, phone number and email address of the person signing up for a free session.

Once you have their email, and their permission, you can continue to market to them over the long-term using your email marketing software in the form of your newsletter, nurture email sequences, or other special offers.

Be patient—it might take someone a year before they decide to call you for a consultation or free session. It's just the long-term nature of building a relationship and trust among your prospects. In the end, it's totally worth it.

I'm not very tech savvy. In the early days of the gym, I tried to delegate my Facebook and Google advertising to a marketing agency to help me out. I thought it would be better to trust the experts. But I had so many bad experiences and wasted a lot of money on the wrong marketing agencies.

Marketing agencies will often start by promising you the world, and it's easy to get swept up in that excitement.

You may soon realize that the marketing agency isn't paying close attention to your account. Most of them have a cookie-cutter approach. I still work with a marketing agency, but I'm very careful, and I watch them like a hawk.

To save yourself cash *and* a headache, always keep these things in mind before running any paid ads.

1. Never pay for ads if you are not tracking everything properly. If you work with a marketing agency, ask them to send you a weekly report showing how much money you spent on ads, how many leads you got from those ads, how many free sessions booked, how many sessions showed up, and how much revenue in deals closed from those ads. Also track which ads performed best and worst. This data will help you make better decisions on your ad spend. For example, if you spend $100 on ads and make back $300, that's a 3X ROI (return on investment), and you know it's safe to increase your spending. But if you are not tracking all of these items above, DO NOT SPEND A PENNY ON ADS!

2. Follow all the rules of the platform and make sure the marketing agency does, too. For example, at the time of this writing, on Facebook, Instagram, and Google you can't use before and after pictures or make any claims in your ads, as that is against their terms. On Facebook and Instagram you also can't use ads to send potential clients to a web page that has before and after pictures or claims, which is why we send them to a simple landing page with an opt-in form instead. Your ad account can be banned for violating the rules. How do I know this? I had to deal with this many times. The agency was too

lazy to pay attention, and I paid the price. When this happened, it took months of appealing to get my ad account back. And in my case I was lucky. Many people do not ever get their ad account back.

3.   Make sure everything you build belongs to you and has been built on your own accounts and with software tools that you own. This ensures that if you stop working with a marketing agency, they won't be able to run off with all of your work, your accounts will keep working, and you will be able to keep track of what's been done before. Having access to this data will help you make smart decisions going forward. This is another lesson I learned the hard way.

4.   Marketing agencies will often act like they know how to run a gym. They will suggest that you change your system, your offer, or your pricing. They might tell you about a book they read or a seminar that taught them this, and they may think they know better than you. Don't fall for it. Trust yourself and trust what I've written in this book. If you do have questions, get advice from someone who runs a successful gym. Reach out to us at SixPax Gym.

PERSONAL IMAGE

When I first came to America, someone gave me a tip about finding a job. He told me to always show up to interviews looking tidy, with clean clothes and clean shoes. He told me it doesn't matter if the clothes are cheap or if they are not brand name—as long as you are tidy and clean, people will know you take care of yourself.

I apply the exact same principle to my gym. People are hiring us, so we must always look good. For my gym, that means not having a scruffy face or untidy hair—unless that's the vibe your gym is going for. Just be aware that how you and your team look sends a message about your branding.

Now that doesn't mean you have to go so far in the opposite direction that your gym feels like a fashion show. It also looks bad if you or your team are constantly checking themselves out in the mirror or obsessed with talking about the latest trends while training a client.

It just means you should look nice and presentable. Look like you take your work and yourself seriously.

I keep it simple. I always wear a SixPax T-shirt or hoodie with simple black pants or shorts with a good pair of shoes.

It's also worth it to make an effort to smell good. Just because you work at a gym doesn't mean you have an excuse to walk around smelling like one! Use deodorant all the time. Keep a couple spare packs at the gym. Brush your teeth.

Me and good boy Milo

Tip: invest in good shoes. You will be standing for long periods of time—I can't emphasize this enough.

NURTURE THOSE LEADS

Once you start to get leads, make sure you follow up with them immediately. Be aggressive. Contact them three times a day via email, calls, and text messages if they have opted in. Answer all of their questions. Text or email them the day before their session to remind them about their training, encourage them, or give them a task.

For example, you should send a message like this before a training session:

"Hi Tami, please come in 10 minutes before your scheduled session so I can weigh you and get your body-fat measurements. Don't forget to write down two days of your diet. See you tomorrow at 5 p.m.!"

You can then send another text in the morning. Something like:

"Good morning, Tami, let's do this! See you at 5 p.m."

Why is this follow up so important? It helps to ensure people will show up to their free session. Caring about these potential new clients enough to remember them and follow up will set you apart from other gyms.

Does the thought of reaching out to clients like this make you nervous? It shouldn't. They need your help. They signed up for a reason, and they just may need a little push. Many clients are dealing with health issues because they procrastinate. It's your job to motivate them.

If they really don't want you to contact them, they can opt out. They aren't held hostage!

CONVERT YOUR LEADS

This is the part most trainers hate! Converting your leads into clients means you have to sell something and get paid.

When I first opened SixPax, I felt guilty asking for money. I have no idea why. Maybe it's because of the way I was raised, or maybe it's because of all the struggles I encountered getting to America. I know there are hundreds of books and doctors who can explain it, but the only thing I thought about was this: if I never got past that guilt, it would be impossible for my business to grow.

You have to get comfortable asking clients to hand over their credit cards. They are paying you for a service.

I have seen so many trainers pour their hearts out, sharing information and explaining the whole program, but they are afraid to ask for payment. Don't be. You deserve to be paid for the work you do. Their lives will change with your training. The money is worth it.

This new client may end up saving money by avoiding junk food and alcohol. They may even be more productive at work, which often translates into earning more income or getting a promotion. I've seen this happen to hundreds of my clients. Be proud of what you are doing and what you are offering.

DELIVERY

This is the part that creates the culture and community of your gym. How are you delivering the service to your clients?

Make sure that every client gets attention. That way they can't cut corners.

Get comfortable calling them out if they try to skip steps, challenge them directly, and encourage them along the way. This shows your clients you care and that you're as invested as they are in their success. It also shows that you aren't just there to make a quick buck.

Your clients will be able to tell if you are half-assing your sessions! Keep your standards high. It's hard, but it's worth it in the end.

Believe me when I say I was so engaged with helping clients I was literally training people in my dreams!

Over the years, I've found that clients love to hear about themselves. Give them feedback. It means a lot to them when you not only point out what they could do better but also what they're doing well. This will pay off in two ways:

1. You will change their lives.

2. You will increase your client retention.

Call your clients by their name while you're training them. People love to hear their names, plus the whole group will start to get to know each other by name. Introduce people to each other at the beginning of sessions, especially new clients.

If you say, "Hi, this is Tami. It's her first day," usually your other clients will be supportive and say something nice. Remember, many clients are nervous and intimidated when they first join. Make them feel like they're at home. Don't push them too hard and keep an eye on them at all times.

RETENTION

The biggest threat to your hustle is losing clients.

Some gym owners are great at getting leads and selling, but they have a problem with retention. They lose clients at a high rate. It's hard to build a community when you see all your clients as temporary bodies in the building.

I didn't have this problem until I got much larger. In the beginning, my delivery was so amazing that I kept clients forever. But as you start to bring on more clients, it becomes harder to pay such individualized attention to all of them. This is why it's so important to create that connection.

If clients do start to leave, you need to figure out why and fix it. In my experience, bad customer service is the number one reason for bad retention.

Here are three tips for improving your retention:

1. Keep following up with them.

2. Send them text messages to ask how they are doing on their diet and cardio.

3. If they miss a session, reach out to them to see what the problem is. You can do this manually at first and then automate it with software as you grow, but you must send a clear message to them that you genuinely care about their progress.

BUILD YOUR VALUE LADDER

Once your incredible marketing strategy gets people to come check out your gym, you can put into practice what I call the value ladder.

You start your offer with the lowest cost and lowest commitment in the beginning. For us at SixPax, that means letting people try a free session.

If we over-deliver value with the free session, they will trust us to take a step up our value ladder and sign up for a paid plan. At the time of this writing, we offer them training twice a week (up to eight sessions) for $299 per month, then when they're ready, we take them to the next level to training three times a week (up to 12 sessions) for $399 per month.

This works well because there is no contract or commitment. Your main goals here are to get the client to show up to the initial free session, and give massive value. You can also include free body fat testing, an eating habit evaluation, cardio tips, and more.

This lets the client try things out. Once they do, they are usually hooked!

Note: These are our prices here in Culver City, California. It's an affluent suburb of Los Angeles, and our clients are successful professionals who have money. Depending on your city and clientele, you may need to adjust your prices accordingly.

BEWARE OF FAKE GURUS

I've noticed many marketers have entered the gym business to help gym owners to grow their gyms. They usually start out helping with lead generation, because many trainers are not good at marketing themselves, then they give advice on how to run a gym. I've even seen marketers run mastermind groups for gym owners on how to run their business. What a shame.

I joined one such group once with the hope of getting help with my marketing automation only to quickly realize the man teaching the class was giving bad advice. He told everyone in the class to hide their prices and have customers call to find out how much something cost. Then he told the class to work to sell them a package according to how the conversation went.

No, no, and another big no!

Doing this is a sure way to start attracting the wrong kind of client. Clients need to know what they're getting into. You shouldn't have to trick or deceive them if they really want your service. And don't you want them to really want your service?

Your phone might not ring as often as you'd like by doing things the right way, but when it does, it will be the right client who is interested. It won't end up being a waste of your time.

I find it strange and dishonest for someone who has never run a gym to try to teach others how to run a gym. Some of those salesmen don't even train. They don't know anything about the gym environment. They treat your gym and personal training like a product—but it's not a product. It's a service.

Many sales pitches are designed to appeal to people's emotions so that they buy something. That might work—at least for the salesperson—when it's a product. But when you sell a service, it can lead to burnout down the road. If you sign up a client who is not a good fit, you still have to deal with them and work with them every time they come in.

You should want to make sure their expectations are realistic. Sit down and set practical goals with them that they can achieve and feel accomplished.

Have you ever joined a program and felt disappointed because it wasn't what you expected? Would you ever do business with them again? Would you ever recommend them? In this situation, who do you think lost the most?

If you have an honest conversation with a potential client, and they decide it isn't the right fit for them, you still have their respect. Even if they don't do business with you in the future, they may gladly refer people to you because they know you do honest business.

If you can't help someone, tell them that. Refer them to someone who can.

Building a reputable gym in your community takes time. There are no shortcuts. You must be honest, dedicated, and consistent. Everything else will follow.

Protect your reputation. I can't emphasize this enough. You are a small gym in your community going against big gyms with a big marketing budget. How will you stand out? By being awesome, over-delivering, and doing honest business.

Another really bad piece of advice I've heard from fake gurus that have never run an actual gym is to give clients what they want, not what they need. What?!

This kind of thinking values money more than anything else, and it's this type of thinking that can give your gym a bad name.

Remember you are building a small gym in your community, a place people come because they trust you and can build a long-term relationship with you. You will train them, their family, and their children—hopefully their grandchildren.

To be honest, most people come in with unrealistic goals because they have been sold fake promises on social media and on TV. Your job is to educate them.

Don't worry about losing a client because you were honest with them. You will be surprised with how many clients appreciate hearing the truth and not some sugar-coated version of it. Of course, don't be rude, but tell them where they stand, point out their weaknesses, tell them the priorities. You are a coach and the expert at what you are prescribing.

We all need people in our lives to be honest with us. For example, I've loved motorcycles all my life and dreamed about having one. Thanks to SixPax Gym, I was finally able to afford one. I went out and bought a big chopper, even though all my friends advised me against it. I wanted to look badass, but it was too big and too fast for my skill level. My friends were right about that. So, I bought a smaller bike and kept practicing until I was confident with the bigger bike.

It's the same with clients. They have an idea, but they don't know it isn't practical. You have to tell them that. When they have unreasonable expectations and don't see those results, reality will hit and they will lose motivation.

Remember, you are going to grow the gym with your story, your commitment, your consistency, and your focus. Be patient, take your time. In Persian we say, "A liar always fools a desperate man!" Do not act desperate because someone will lie to you. Do not fall for fake promises from fake gurus who have never run a gym.

CHAPTER 34

CARVE OUT YOUR MARKET

I thought it would be difficult to sell 30-minute sessions, but to my surprise people loved it! It worked perfectly for my clientele, who are mainly busy professionals who don't have hours to spend at the gym. They were looking for a short, intense workout, and that's exactly what I gave them.

In order to find more clients through marketing, I had to learn more about my market! I got to know my clients, learned what they do for a living, how many kids they have, and how far from the gym they work. I have interviewed hundreds of clients to find out why they joined me. Why Six-Pax and not a gym down the street? What makes them keep coming back?

You don't need to have your market totally figured out in the beginning. It's good to have an idea of who will come to your gym, but sometimes what's on paper doesn't work in the real world. If things don't work out like you expect, don't panic. The market will respond, and you can change your course accordingly.

It's constant work, and that's the beauty of it—kind of like bodybuilding itself! There is always something you'll be able to improve. Even eight-time Mr. Olympia Ronnie Coleman, at the top of his game, wanted to be better and make improvements. That being said, when you find something that works, do not change the recipe.

I didn't realize it at first, but offering only 30-minute sessions made it easier for me to get clients to pay, too. It was harder to convince them to pay for a full hour, but they were fine with paying for 30 minutes because busy professionals are always short on time. The offer looked attractive and valuable, clients got results, and I got paid.

Trainer testimony: *Miles Nightingale*

My name is Miles Nightingale, and I am a trainer here at SixPax Gym.

Initially finding out about this adult Disneyland through my high school football team was the best thing that has ever happened to me. With the mindset of putting on strength and muscle mass for my athletic performance and overall fitness goals, SixPax did exactly that. Turning myself from 185 to 210 pounds of solid muscle in no time. Not only that, but meeting all the amazing warriors and building relationships along the way.

My commitment towards the gym caused my results to amplify. Day in day out. After several months of pushing myself to the limit inside the gym and out, money became tight due to me being young and in school with lots of priorities at 16 years of age. That's when I proposed to the boss himself (Siavash) to clean the gym and assist with maintenance in return for training. That's how much I cared and how driven I was. After discussing this with Siavash himself, he was all for it. Me being 16 at the time, offering a service in return for a membership impressed Siavash through my courage, confidence and ambition to reach my goals.

He then started showing his love and caring efforts to me and I began learning everything! From closing clients, scheduling, training clients and just running a business in general. I was able to do it all. My energy and passion mixed with my knowledge through fitness, nutrition and living a healthy balanced lifestyle got me a spot as an official Athletic/fitness Coach at SixPax Gym. Now almost three years later as a coach I am all gas forward. Continuing to change lives, inspire, motivate and push people to be the best version of themselves is what my life consists of on a daily basis and will continue to be so moving forward.

I am with this Gym for life and plan on owning my own SixPax very soon. The love for this gym won't ever change. Constantly growing and improving in the most successful small gym in America.

Miles Nightingale

Coach "No Mercy" Miles

CHAPTER 35

BUILDING THE RIGHT TEAM

When I started SixPax, I didn't have staff. I just worked seven days a week from 6 a.m. to 8 p.m. to keep the gym going. I never took a day off. I even worked Christmas and New Year's.

I couldn't hire anyone in the beginning because I couldn't pay them. Plus, I didn't know how any of that worked with taxes and liability (see Chapter 24).

That all changed when I met a client named Peri. He joined the gym because he couldn't gain weight. He was skinny and tall, and he always rode his bicycle to the gym. He was such a hard-working guy! He always showed up for his training sessions and he stayed true to the diet. I got him ready for a competition and he looked amazing. We were all excited about him competing because that was his dream.

The day before the show, he told me his employer didn't let him take days off—not even one. If he tried, his employer would fire him. I was so mad and furious for him! He worked so hard—he deserved a break every now and then.

"You need to find a better job," I told him. "What is your dream job?"

"I would love to be a trainer someday," he said.

Even though it was a leap for me, I liked Peri, so I hired him. At that point, I didn't trust anyone else to train my clients, but I hired him to keep the doors open while I took a lunch break.

Coach Peri

I had a hard time not jumping in to correct him all the time at first, but eventually we both learned how to do the job! He was so solid. He always showed up on time, was always polite, and had a great work ethic. Peri began to work his way up, and he is now my gym manager. He's been with me for nine years.

I thought everyone I'd hire would be like Peri, but I was wrong. In the beginning, I didn't have a good hiring process, so I hired a lot of people who were wrong for the job. Many of them quit or just did their own thing. A friend of mine eventually told me the key was to hire true believers, and suddenly it clicked.

I began hiring people from within the SixPax community itself, and the results were amazing! They believed in what SixPax stood for, they had the experience firsthand, and they knew what kind of difference SixPax could make in people's lives.

Along the way, I learned a few things. Hiring people is hard but having a team that is too lean is even harder. This will burn out good employees and the quality of your service will suffer. I always look for these characteristics when I'm hiring:

- → Do they enjoy fitness?

- → Do they enjoy training and being in a gym environment?

- → Do they believe in my system?

- → Do they know anything about SixPax and my story?

- → Do they enjoy helping others?

- → Are they outgoing?

- → Are they ambitious?

To figure out what kind of hire I need to make, I like to conduct time studies to pinpoint where I'm spending most of my time and how I can delegate that work to someone who can do it even better than me. Then I can hire someone to fill that specific need.

But the bottom line is they have to believe in the mission. I can train people to be able to train others, but I am always looking for true believers.

Once you hire the right people, you can start to build a real team.

INTERVIEWING POTENTIAL TRAINERS

How many interviews should you have? What questions should you ask? You should document these ahead of time.

We have three interviews with each candidate. I conduct the last interview.

Each time a new person joins our team, we have an onboarding process. I help them get the necessary certifications, depending on the position, to protect me and my business from liability.

JOB DESCRIPTIONS

Before you hire a new employee, it's important to write out a clear description of each position so that your new hire will know what their duties are and what is expected from them. The description should include the role, responsibility, results, and requirements for each job. Every position has a job description, even mine as CEO.

Here is an example of my job description for a head coach:

Job Description

Role, Responsibilities, Results, Requirements

Position:	Head Coach
Department:	Training
Reports To:	CEO/Founder (Siavash Fashi)
Job Type:	SixPax Gym

Summary: At SixPax Gym, we offer 30 minutes of high interval fitness training guaranteed to deliver results. Our business is growing fast, and we are looking for head coaches to help support our growth.

Role and Responsibilities

Classes

→ Lead semi-private class sessions of predesigned SixPax system interval training.

→ Deliver a consistent high-intensity training session experience for all clients and guests.

→ Manage efficient class flow with varying abilities, including delegating clear direction to clients and assistant coaches during weightlifting activities.

→ Always start and end 30-minute classes promptly.

→ Watch for and quickly correct exercise form to prevent injuries.

→ Help new and returning clients and guests feel welcome and motivated!

Outside of Classes

→ Answer phone inquiries and follow up with new leads (within a five-minute timeframe).

→ Check in with current clients to keep them accountable.

→ Sign up new clients and complete light admin work to input their information into our system.

→ Attend regular team meetings and training.

Results (Expected Accomplishments)

→ Every client walks away spent and satisfied.

→ Maintain current customer retention.

→ Help continue to grow our roster of awesome clientele.

Requirements (Expected Proficiencies)

→ Friendly and open demeanor—we really mean this. Authenticity is one of our core values, and we have a small team.

→ Being able to lift a minimum of 50 pounds.

→ Certifications after one month of SixPax training experience.

→ Basic computer knowledge using Windows and Excel.

→ Genuine interest in helping clients reach their fitness goals.

→ Excellent verbal communication skills for initiating and maintaining professional relationships with clients.

→ Able to multitask in a highly fast paced work environment.

→ Open to coaching and receiving feedback.

→ Must be open to trial runs/auditions prior to hiring as part of interview process.

→ A naturally energetic personality is a huge plus!

THE IMPORTANCE OF TRANSPARENCY

One of the biggest things you can do as a gym owner is learn to manage and lead people with transparency. This means communicating with your whole team openly and honestly and encouraging them to do the same.

This kind of culture is only possible if it starts from the top down, which means you are responsible for creating it.

Share with your team exactly what's going on in the business—this means the good and the bad. Share your revenue numbers and the big goals of the company. The more honest you are, the more your team will trust you and work hard to make your goals their goals.

How do you do this?

Like I mentioned earlier, start every workday with a morning meeting. It doesn't have to be long. Even 5 to 10 minutes will work. This will give the whole team a chance to talk about any important updates, problems, or solutions. Go over your critical number—this is how many paid clients you have in the system that day.

At first I was afraid for my team to know how many clients we had or how much revenue we were bringing in. But my mentor said, "They already know. They can do the math." Once I began sharing everything, my team made it their mission to drive even harder. Many were shocked because most businesses hide the revenue from their employees, but when you include them, it motivates them to push for that success, like a football team winning the Super Bowl.

Second, as a leader, you must be willing to share with your team and ask for honest feedback. The more you model this behavior, the more your team will buy into it. It will make your whole team more open to giving and receiving feedback. It may feel uncomfortable at times, but it will help your team and your gym grow and improve.

Third, trust your team. Too many leaders out there today micromanage their teams because they don't trust their teams to do their jobs. But if you don't trust your people, why hire them? Instead of telling everyone what to do all the time, tell your team the outcome that you expect from them. You expect that clients are satisfied. You expect the gym to be clean. You expect trainers to be focused during each session. Let them own those results.

DAILY MEETINGS

Every day we have a quick meeting in the morning, which also has a process.

We have built a structure for it. One of the team members runs the meeting, and if he is sick or busy, another team member will take over and run the meeting with the same framework. Nothing changes. Our system does not depend on anyone—including me.

That meeting is very simple. We greet each other. We go over any critical issues (usually there are none), any announcements, and then we review our critical number: how many paid clients we have. And then we go on with our day. This may seem like a meaningless exercise, but it's actually one of the most important processes we have. It connects the entire team and helps us all to work toward the same goal, which is increasing the number of paid clients.

My monthly financial process is documented, too. Every month I get a report from my bookkeeper on an Excel spreadsheet that I have built to highlight the important numbers, such as gross profit, net profit, payroll, and expenses. This allows me to evaluate the business and compare each month with the previous month or year to track our growth.

Here is an example of our monthly key metrics:

Critical Number (Paid Clients)
Profitability
Gross Revenue
Gross Expenses
Gross Profit
Expenses
Marketing Expense
Gym Expense
Subscription Expense
Payroll Expense

Critical Number (Paid Clients)
Clients
Total Leads
Clients Joined
Clients Terminated
FT Team
Team Members Added
Team Members Removed
Total Team Headcount

NO GOSSIP POLICY

There are very few universal policies I recommend to everyone, but I firmly believe a no-gossip policy is critical. Gossip destroys organizations, hurts morale, and can make it impossible for team members to get their work done.

Problems should always be taken to someone in leadership, to someone who can help, someone who can solve them.

Most small businesses just accept gossip as a given. But the problem is when people start talking about each other, the rumor mill gets started. Things get exaggerated. You stop getting the results you want. It's poison.

Your main goal should be to build up a team and delegate everything you do, so you can pull yourself out of the day-to-day operations of the gym and focus on where you're going. A no-gossip policy is critical to building up a healthy team that will allow you to do this.

Here's my challenge to you: A no-gossip policy has to start with you. Don't talk about clients to the people around you. Only talk to the people who can actually solve the problem. Don't talk about people in front of your team. This is one of the hardest things I've had to learn as a CEO. If you expect your team to follow a policy, it has to start with you. Live by those rules and you will see a significant improvement in your workplace culture.

Building a solid team is key to your growth, so keep working on it, and never give up!

FIRING AN EMPLOYEE

In the beginning, I didn't have a process for hiring my employees. I just went with my gut. I got lucky with a couple of my hires, but eventually my luck ran out. I hired one of my clients—he was passionate about training and loved the gym style. He claimed he was a boxer and could teach kick-boxing cardio classes, so I hired him.

I invested a bunch of money building a rack and buying boxing gloves and boxing bags. He started running the classes, and I noticed he didn't know much about training people. Clients started to complain that their wrists hurt, so I began to suspect he didn't know how to coach them.

I didn't want to give up on him because I felt responsible for him. This was his only source of income, so I started training him to become a personal trainer. Things only got worse. He started poisoning the team with gossip, bumming rides from clients, and even trying to borrow money from clients. It was terrible. Plus, he made too many mistakes on the floor—mistakes that could put the clients in danger and injure them.

I finally sat down with him one day to talk about his performance. I asked if I could support him in any way, but he said that he was overwhelmed and wanted to start driving for Uber instead.

So, I wished him luck in his new career.

I had him sign a release waiver that one of my clients, a lawyer, drafted for me. He signed it, and I gave him $1,000 plus his wages. We parted ways, and he thanked me for all the help.

Even if it seems like a firing went well, you need to be prepared for that to change.

Six months later I received a letter from that former employee's lawyer trying to shake me down for money. The lawyer claimed I treated his client—my former employee—unfairly and that he shouldn't have been fired.

I was shocked and scared. I didn't know how to respond. It was then I started to realize how bad things could go for me without documentation. I didn't have a process for keeping any written documentation of him not being able to do his job.

I spoke to my friend Daniel about this. He oversees many employees, and he told me to contact an employment lawyer right away, hand the lawyer all the paperwork, and let the professional deal with it. His main advice was to hire someone who was qualified to do the work and not to try to take any shortcuts.

I hired a lawyer for $500 an hour. I couldn't believe how expensive it was, but I sent her all the paperwork.

She told me the waiver I made him sign was the only chance I had to fight this. She started corresponding with the other lawyer, and he dropped the claim. I spent a couple of thousand dollars, but it was money well spent! I started working with her to have all my hiring processes, employee manual, and documentation brought up to date and made sure they were state compliant.

This doesn't mean you won't have any issues with employees, but it will give you comfort knowing you are protected.

I had to fire another employee who was nothing but dramatic. She was always late to work, was rude to clients, and talked about her personal drama with clients. She had a million excuses for not doing her job, so I let her go. I even gave her two weeks of pay. Two months later, I received a letter from a lawyer asking for documents and text messages about the firing. Right away I contacted my lawyer. This time I was prepared.

I had all the necessary paperwork documenting all the infractions to show I was following the laws and regulations of my state. Again, the claim was dropped because I was prepared.

You must have a process for firing employees.

Even before you consider firing someone, make sure all your communications are documented.

I have many conversations with employees about their performance, and we talk about things that need to be improved. Document those conversations. If they don't improve, and the employee continues to make those same mistakes, you will have a record of it. This will help protect you from any possible lawsuits.

If you don't keep a record of those conversations, it will be hard to show how you came to the conclusion you needed to let this person go.

Most of the time, firings happen because of poor communication. CEOs are often not clear about what they are expecting from an employee, meaning the employee is not set up for success.

As a CEO, it's your job to train and educate your employees. Do your part and do it well. If you learn an employee is not a good fit, let them go. Make it short, be nice, and be respectful.

It will be emotional, so make sure you don't drag out the process. Don't try to soften the blow by suggesting they may apply again in the future. Just tell them you are going in a different direction and thank them for the work they've done.

WORKPLACE COMPLIANCE

I also have a process for protecting SixPax by having my team take training about sexual-harassment, diversity and inclusion, and more. In many states this is required. I use a service called Traliant. It's inexpensive. You can check their website www.traliant.com for more information.

Trainer testimonial: *Miles Concepcion*

Before I worked at SixPax, I was quiet, for the most part. I thought of myself as shy and reserved. For years, I worked to make myself better as an athlete and student but would rarely have enough confidence to share my skills with the world. As soon as I started working at SixPax Gym, my life changed. Training and exercising were no longer about one person. My knowledge now had to be expressed to the public with most, if not all, of them being professionals in their careers. I was still a teenager, and some of them were decades older than me. This made me very timid in the first few months of the job. I used to have entire classes where I may have only said one word. But after being guided and mentored by Siavash and Bill, I learned to raise my voice and have more self-confidence in my craft. I was no longer the timid lifter—I became my own professional. I can now coach entire classes on my own, confidently. This also applies to outside the gym. I can now express myself with confidence and pride in any environment. Working as an assistant coach has changed me forever and made me a more mentally, emotionally, and physically strong human being.

CHAPTER 36

CUSTOMER SERVICE

When it comes to being a great trainer and a gym owner, customer service and experience are keys to making sure your clients are satisfied every time they walk through your doors.

I've found that one of the best ways to make sure your clients have a quality experience is to make sure that experience is always the same. That means you have to make sure your clients have that same kind of interaction, whether it's you or your employees greeting them. Consistency is the key to success.

FIRST IMPRESSIONS

It all starts with a first smile and a warm welcome.

Remember that your attitude and your actions leave an impression on your clients. Always keep your word. If you say you will text them, make sure you do! Always speak loud and clear. Make sure to listen, listen, listen.

GET THE RIGHT CUSTOMERS

Over the years, I've learned that one percent of your clients will give you 99 percent of your headaches. I've also learned it's okay to get rid of problem clients. In the beginning, I was desperate for money, so I trained everyone I possibly could. Some of them were so rude that every time I saw their name on the schedule, it would mess up my day. I knew I had to deal with these people and put on a happy face, but inside I hated training them. Still, I gave them the best service possible because they paid me money. But so many of them were unreasonably demanding or would even try to cheat me during sessions or cancel at the last minute.

One day I was pissed at a client for trying to cheat me. I was still in a bad mood when my client, friend, and successful businessman named Dennis came in.

He could tell something was off that day, so he asked if I was okay. I told him what happened and why I was upset. Immediately, he turned around and told me to just get rid of that client.

"Look at your situation," he said. "His behavior is making you mad, and your attitude is affecting the good clients!"

Until then, I hadn't fully realized I had that option. I quickly got rid of that client and it felt amazing.

Now, of course, I didn't drag that client out kicking and screaming and slam the door in his face, even if a part of me really wanted to do that. There is a right way to handle bad clients, and bad employees for that matter. Cut ties with them politely and systematically so there are no hard feelings.

But the bottom line is, you shouldn't be afraid to refuse or get rid of bad clients so you can focus on the good clients.

I once had a client who, no matter how much attention we paid her, always complained. She didn't like how the trainers talked and used phrases like, "Five more," "You got this," "Power," or "Squeeze." She often complained she had shoulder, back, and knee issues, which made it impossible to train her in a way that would work for her since our training style uses free weights and an aggressive approach to get results.

I sat down with her and apologized for her experience. I suggested she train at another gym that had more equipment and work with a specialized trainer so she could work around her injuries and meet her goals. Then, I refunded her the full amount, even though she had trained with us for a month.

She thanked me and left.

Ultimately, SixPax wasn't the best fit for her. By letting her know that rather than dragging out the process, we were able to part on good terms.

THE CUSTOMER ALWAYS COMES FIRST

Once you cultivate a good group of clients who embody your culture, you must work to keep them. It's important to personalize your approach and make sure they know that you know who they are. Prove you appreciate them. You can start by making sure to address them by name each time you communicate with them.

ALWAYS GIVE YOUR BEST, PLUS MORE

You should train your employees to go the extra mile for your customers. Teach them to be respectful and kind at all times. This can go a long way toward improving your business's customer service record. Remember, it's often these little things that make a big difference to customers. Have a mindset that makes it clear to your customers that no request is too small to be considered. Also, never let your customers think you are guilty of favoritism.

DELICATE SITUATIONS

If a client complains, don't get angry. You can use this opportunity to learn from them how you can improve your gym. Also, it's not easy to complain. If they're doing so, it means something really bothered them. Show them that you're listening, you care, and you want to do something about it. Make them feel good, not guilty, for sharing their thoughts with you.

At the same time, be careful to never change major parts of your business based on a complaint of one loud client. You need to weigh decisions carefully before turning your business upside down.

I also recommend you keep healthy boundaries between you and your clients. Only give advice about the training and tips you're getting paid for. Stay away from life lessons, relationship tips, religious opinions, or political opinions. And never ever, ever date your clients (or employees for that matter). Steer clear of this to avoid costly legal trouble.

Never argue about sessions or try to prove to a client that they're wrong or that they're lying. Always offer a fair resolution. If a client asks for a refund, give them the refund immediately without hesitation. Don't make them feel guilty. It's better for your reputation if you handle those situations well.

NEVER LEAVE ISSUES UNRESOLVED

Every complaint must be addressed. I do follow-up calls or talk to clients in person to make sure that all complaints have been resolved. Do not simply react—take your time. Sometimes clients are having a bad day and need a little space and time. Tell them you are here to help and that you value their business. Let them empty their hearts out to you. By doing this, you'll learn a lot about what's going on at your gym. Explain to them how you're going to fix the problem, give them a date to follow up with them, and tell them about the progress you've made.

AS YOU TRAIN

As you train them, make sure you are firm and honest with your clients. Don't make them feel guilty about anything, but be honest about their progress and help them improve. Forgive their setbacks and restart as many times as you need. That's why they're paying you!

Highlight their successes and celebrate their accomplishments. You can do this by giving out awards. Don't give out false praise, and if they are slacking, remind them why they joined your gym in the first place. Encourage them to get back on track.

Be firm but flexible. Work around other people's schedules. As much as possible, make the gym a place where people don't have to stress out. The gym should be a stress reliever.

Be vulnerable with your clients. It's okay to show them you aren't perfect.

If you make a mistake and people notice it, acknowledge it and learn from it. You're a trainer, but you're also a human—you will make mistakes, and you do have limitations.

Start every class off with a positive sentence, such as "Let's kill it!" or "Let's get this party started!" Feel free to make up your own.

Why Does Customer Service Matter?

If you do a great job with customer service, you will have repeat business. You invest a lot of money on ads, websites, signs, and more to get clients. Do you really want to lose those clients because they didn't like the experience? No! You must figure out how to keep them.

You can't make everyone happy, so it's inevitable that some clients will leave because they just aren't a good match for the culture of your gym. That doesn't mean you should make it easier for them to leave by being rude, being late to sessions, or ignoring them. Be nice and provide the very best service until the end.

TRAINING FOR CUSTOMER SERVICE

You might have all kinds of ideas about what great customer service looks like. But does your team understand your vision? Do they know how to execute it? While it's important to understand the huge impact that great customer service can have on your gym, it's also important to train your team to be up to the challenge.

Step 1: Customer Service Training

Be an example. You must practice what you preach and treat your clients and employees with respect. Always speak politely about people—your employees are watching what you do. Give them concrete examples of acceptable and unacceptable behavior and the steps they should take in various situations. Give them a clear list of dos and don'ts.

For example, I teach my employees that, when they are training people, they should always position themselves in a way that doesn't make the client uncomfortable. Don't square off—us trainers are muscular, and that can make people feel intimidated. You can work on making people feel comfortable by always greeting them when they walk in, calling them by their first time, being supportive and encouraging, and staying away from politics and religion.

Help your employees understand why offering good customer service is important to the business and how it will ultimately impact them. Employees are motivated to improve their customer service skills if they believe doing so will be beneficial to them, too.

Prepare scripts for common customer service issues. This will help to ensure that your customer service team will be able to deliver a speedy and uniform responses.

For example, if a client asks for a refund, we have a simple script we send out through text or email that generally reads like this:

"Thank you for training with us. I will take care of it now. Please allow your bank five business days to process the refund. Keep up the great work!"

If a new lead comes in, we have a script that reads like this:

"Thanks for reaching out! I would be more than happy to help you. Please let me know when you are available so I can schedule your free session."

Step 2: Ensure Your Team Gives Consistent, Quality Service

Have your team document all conversations with clients. Keep a track of all text and email messages. Reply to clients within five minutes if it's a simple task.

For example, if a client asks for a schedule change, reply within five minutes. "Can I try a free session?" Reply within five minutes.

This sends a signal that you are proud of what you do, and you know it's important.

BE A GOOD ROLE MODEL

Remember, all the training in the world won't matter if you aren't treating your employees well. The way you treat them will be how they treat your customers. You are their role model, so always be the epitome of a good service provider.

Greet your employees enthusiastically every day and listen when they speak. Foster a positive culture. I always try to thank my employees at the end of the day in front of the clients and acknowledge their hard work and importance to the gym. I have noticed how much people respect me for that. They always thank me for taking good care of my employees.

Never forget this: Your employees are your clients too.

CHAPTER 37

YOUR NEXT MOVE

> **66** *The more I help others to succeed, the more I succeed.*[14]
>
> — RAY KROC

During my first five years in America, I couldn't afford to go to the doctor to check on my eye cancer. So much has changed since then.

When I opened SixPax Gym, I was just a young man with a dream. As Six-Pax grew, I had no choice but to grow along with it. I spent so many sleepless nights full of doubts, fear of failure, and excitement. As my hard work started to pay off, one of the first things I did was buy a muscle car. I realize now that it wasn't a smart investment, and since then I've learned a lot about finances—but coming from extreme poverty, I was always dreaming about fancy cars, so at that time it made me feel like I had finally made it.

Because I had elevated myself from having an all cash under-the-table business and had years of tax returns showing well documented income, I was able to buy myself a three-bedroom house with a two-car garage a short distance the beach. It even has a built-in gym. I remodeled my house and made it exactly the way I wanted it. Parked in front is my Harley and a big truck with the SixPax logo on it. I drive them around loud and proud! I ride my Harley on the Pacific Coast Highway, looking at the water and dreaming about a better future. And of course, I have good health insurance.

Training my good friend and mentor, Daniel, in my garage at home

I came to America searching for the American dream, just like Arnold, and now I'm living it.

I wake up in the morning, drink my coffee, make six whole eggs, and start my day. I get to enjoy my breakfast, knowing SixPax Gym opened up at 6 a.m. and is running like a machine. I know my trainers are taking care of our clients and pushing them to their limits.

I write my goals for the day and jump in my monster truck to head to the gym. It's just a few minutes from my house.

When I arrive, I get to see the gym and my clients training hard. Everyone has a smile on their face. I get a sincere "Good morning" greeting from everyone. I'm happy to be at SixPax. I can't imagine myself being anywhere else. I go to the office to check on all the new sign-ups. I respond to all my emails.

If the people in my community don't know my name, they for sure know my face, and they know about SixPax. I remember the days when I didn't have any friends in this country. No one cared about my hopes or my dreams then, but SixPax changed all that.

After 20 years of being away from home, I was even able to sponsor my parents to come visit me in America. I bought a house for them in Iran, and my parents live there rent-free. I help my sisters and my brothers whenever they need it. I always find myself buying gifts for my nephews and sending them to Iran. I love being able to see the big smiles on their faces when I'm able to surprise them like that. I am able to do more charity and help friends back home who are struggling.

My family may have doubted my path in the beginning, but they have a new respect for me now and all that I have been able to accomplish. My father, who was critical of me when I was younger, is now proud of me and listens to what I have to say.

My vision is clear. I believe in myself and in my ability. I've figured out how to make the most of my time and appreciate what life has to offer.

When I was in Iran, I thought life was a punishment. I grew up believing we were put on earth to suffer. Now I know better. Life is a gift!

For this book, I asked a few of my employees to write a testimonial about how SixPax changed their lives, and what they said brought tears to my eyes. Some called me a role model. Some called me a father figure. Some said they wanted to be like me and open their own gym someday.

I still can't believe I've had that kind of impact on people. I can't believe my life every time I walk into my house or go out to eat at a nice restaurant.

I'm a free man, and I make decisions like one.

I know that even if I win the lottery tonight, you'll still be seeing me at Six-Pax tomorrow morning. Every Saturday, I still sit inside the gym alone after everyone has done their sessions. I close the door and count my blessings.

I have built the most successful small gym in America.

I developed the perfect model for small gyms—one that is simple and effective. I have figured out every part of this business through trial and error, and I have created a method and a process that has helped thousands of people look and feel amazing.

If you are passionate about helping others, few things change lives more than helping people through fitness and giving them the gift of health.

Our gym environment is positive and inspiring. Everyone wants to better themselves. Our clients are so appreciative of what we do, and in return, we can see the kind of impact we have on them. That makes this business so rewarding.

The SixPax method is a proven system. You don't have to waste time trying to figure this out on your own. Take this wisdom and just execute it!

In a gym that takes up less than 1,000 square feet, SixPax brings in more than $1 million a year, and we are changing lives daily. What else could I ask for? I am living the dream!

I want to help you live yours, too. This can be you.

This book is a great start, and I hope it helps give you direction as you get started in the fitness industry.

SixPax Gym is much bigger than me. It's my duty to grow SixPax as much as I can to help more people. My goal is to change as many lives as I can, and my plan for that is by training others to start, run, and grow their own small gyms in the most effective way possible.

If my book has inspired you, and you would like to take the next step to building your own profitable fitness business, visit www.sixpaxgym.com/gymbuilders.

ACKNOWLEDGMENTS

This book is a culmination of a long and arduous journey. No one reaches any success alone, and I have many people I would like to thank:

Daniel Rosen for mentoring me and changing my life.

Ostad Omidfar, my Taekwondo teacher for 7 years since I was eight years old, you taught me discipline.

Mehdi Abassi Nejad for showing me Arnold's picture for the first time when I was 16 years old.

Arnold Schwarzenegger for inspiring me to become a bodybuilder and come to America.

Joe Weider for spreading stories of successful and larger than life characters. I want to be one of them.

Dorian Yates for teaching me intensity and commitment and setting an example for how a gym should look and feel. When I trained at Temple Gym, there was no way I could enjoy training anywhere else—it was simple and intense.

Max B. Chester, the amazing young lawyer who fought so hard for my freedom while I was in prison.

Peter Longwood for being one of my first friends in Los Angeles. He mentored me like a father figure, gave me life advice, took me to Gold's gym (which gave me confidence because everyone knew I was with him), and trained me in bodybuilding for years without charging me a penny. Thank you for all of your kindness and wisdom.

Dave Palumbo, my nutritionist, for teaching me how the body works and how to manipulate my nutrition to get powerful results.

Alex Charfen, thank you for teaching me how to build a simple operation at my gym and scale my business.

Grant Mitchell, my amazing landlord, for taking a chance and believing in me, treating me so well, and for all the support to my business and dreams.

Messrob Torikian, my first client who joined the gym and still trains at the same time after 11 years, 7:30 am warrior.

My friend and client Dennis Lunder for all of your amazing business advice.

My friend Gautam Shenoy for all your support and encouragement.

Vincent West for lending me $375 to buy my first set of dumbbells for the gym.

Keenan Jones for your continued help and inspiration with our SixPax marketing technology and strategy.

Hossein Alamir for educating me on finances.

ACKNOWLEDGMENTS

Tom Platz for training me and self belief that was installed in me. I will never forget those three-hour leg training sessions at Gold's Gym.

Johnny Traynor, my coach who always gives me honest feedback. When I trained with Johnny, I knew I had to be on time: 1 min. late and you are in big trouble. I left my house Saturday morning from LA to be at World's Gym in San Diego at 8 a.m. to train legs with him. I left one hour early, because if I was late he would have attitude, and that's not good on leg day. One year of training every Saturday, an amazing time of my life.

Coach Goodyear (Rest In Peace) from Culver City High School for sending all the football players from Culver City High School to me. I helped them and trained most of the key players. The team finally won the CIF championship for the first time in 40 years.

Shari Schreiber for helping me to break patterns and understand myself better, teaching me life is a reflection myself.

All the SixPax warriors at the gym who are supporting SixPax.

My amazing SixPax team: my right hand man, Peri Boszko, for being by my side through thick and thin, helping me to build SixPax Gym from nothing; Operations Manager Mark James; Coach "Big Bill" Tenwick; Coach Eroll David; Assistant Coach "Strong" Miles Concepcion; and Assistant Coach "No Mercy" Miles Nightingale for working hard, supporting my vision, and helping to change thousands of lives.

SixPax cardio kickboxing coaches Jason Murphy, Kahlil Joseph, and Remana King.

Kelly Regan from BookLaunchers for your amazing work in helping me to articulate and deliver my message in this book.

Julie Broad CEO of BookLaunchers for creating a place for people like myself to tell their story.

ENDNOTES

1   Diane Disney Miller, as told to Pete Martin, *The Story of Walt Disney* (New York: Holt, 1957).

2   Rhonda Byrne, *The Secret* (New York: Atria Books, 2006).

3   Ray Kroc, "Ray Kroc Interview," YouTube video, May 12, 2017, https://www.youtube.com/watch?v=3cBv8jBTAs4.

4   Will Smith, "Will Smith and Tina Fey," *Oprah* (Chicago: Harpo Studios, November 6, 2008).

5   A. M. Mannion, "Domestication and the Origins of Agriculture: An Appraisal," *Progress in Physical Geography: Earth and Environment* 23, iss. 1 (March 1, 1999): 37-56.

6   "Heart Disease Facts," Centers for Disease Control and Prevention, accessed August 21, 2022, https://www.cdc.gov/heartdisease/facts.htm#:~:text=Heart%20disease%20is%20the%20leading,groups%20in%20the%20United%20States.&text=One%20person%20dies%20every%2034,United%20States%20from%20cardiovascular%20disease.&text=About%20697%2C000%20people%20in%20the,1%20in%20every%205%20deaths.

7   Ibid.

8   "American Cancer Society Guideline for Diet and Physical Activity," American Cancer Society, accessed August 21, 2022, https://www.cancer.org/healthy/eat-healthy-get-active/acs-guidelines-nutrition-physical-activity-cancer-prevention/guidelines.html.

9   "Overweight & Obesity Statistics," National Institute of Diabetes and Digestive and Kidney Diseases, accessed August 21, 2022, https://www.niddk.nih.gov/health-information/health-statistics/overweight-obesity#:~:text=Fast%20Facts&text=Nearly%201%20in%203%20adults%20(30.7%25)%20are%20overweight.&text=More%20than%202%20in%205%20adults%20(42.4%25)%20

have%20obesity.&text=About%201%20in%2011%20adults%20(9.2%25)%20
have%20severe%20obesity.

10 Ibid.

11 Brad Stone, *The Everything Store: Jeff Bezos and the Age of Amazon* (New York: Little, Brown and Company, 2013).

12 Brian Dakss, "4 in 5 Credit Reports Have Errors," CBS News, October 12, 2004, https://www.cbsnews.com/news/4-in-5-credit-reports-have-errors/.

13 "Starbucks Principles For Upholding the Third Place: For Our Partners, Our Customers and Our Communities," Starbucks, January 24, 2019, https://stories.starbucks.com/press/2019/starbucks-principles-for-upholding-the-third-place-for-our-partners-our-customers-and-our-communities/.

14 Attributed to Ray Kroc.